Postcolonial Perspectives

English South African Fiction Under Apartheid

Ann Clayton

Clayton, Ann
    Postcolonial Perspectives: English South African
    Fiction Under Apartheid / Ann Clayton

Criticism.

ISBN: (pbk) 978-1-928171-63-8
ISBN: (ebk) 978-1-928171-64-5

Copyright © Ann Clayton, 2017

Cover image is "Icarus" by David Wilhelm

Vocamus Community Publications

130 Dublin Street North
Guelph, Ontario
N1H 4N4

Contents

Preface		1
Chapter 1.	Citizens and Subjects, Country and Town	4
Chapter 2.	Rereading South African Culture in the Post-Colony	13
Chapter 3.	Gender and Narrative: Olive Schreiner and Pauline Smith	28
Chapter 4.	Plaatje's *Mhudi*: Ambivalent Alliances and African Humanism	50
Chapter 5.	Desire and Transgression: Nationalism, Degeneracy and the 'Miscegenation Novel'	62
Chapter 6.	Novels of Colonial and Postcolonial Migrancy: Alan Paton, Peter Abrahams, Nadine Gordimer	82
Chapter 7.	Petrified Gardens and the River of Life: Versions of Anti-pastoral	94
Chapter 8.	Re-reading Resistance: La Guma, Serote, Sepamla	105
Chapter 9.	Nationalism, Postcolonialism, and the Politics of Representation: Lauretta Ngcobo's *And They Didn't Die*	119
Chapter 10.	"Postmodernism of the Homeless": Racial and Sexual Politics in Nadine Gordimer's *None to Accompany Me*	136
Notes		148
Selected Bibliography		161
Biographical Note		186

Preface

This overview of the South African novel grew out of the reading I did while working on short pieces for encyclopedias, and in order to teach a graduate course in South African fiction at the University of Guelph, Ontario. I have attempted to lay down the main lines of development and the key turning points in the English South African novel. I have given emphasis to political crises in order to highlight the connections between political history and fiction, assuming the development of socio-political history has had significant bearing on the production and reception of fiction. My context is that of an ex-South African critic and teacher of literature now living and working in Canada. Thus I have also taken 1994, the year of the first democratic election in South Africa, as a terminal point for my discussion of the main novels written during the apartheid era.

My aims in this book were to politicize postcolonial critique more fully by relating South African novels to their political and historical moment . In particular, I wanted to show that it is in the relationship between competing nationalisms and state formations that the significance of cultural interventions is to be found. I also wished to show that gender has been a dimension of analysis often lacking in previous studies of South African fiction, and gender has been inadequately related to the politics of race, class, and cultural production. Now that citizenship has been given to all South Africans in the form of the franchise, it has become clearer that the lack of citizenship and political voice has affected the literary production of women, racial minorities, and the black majority at different phases of South African history. I also wished to show relationships among colonialism, gender, language and narrative form as they have been articulated differently at different historical conjunctures.

Given that the changes in the nineties have been so radical and wide-ranging, with the establishment of a multi-racial democracy, I thought it would be useful to move away from the binary thinking that characterized critical thought in the apartheid era. I also wished to show resistance in the making, the unfolding of black consciousness fiction, particularly as these texts have often been dismissed as propaganda or as superficial documentation of racial oppression. It also seemed important to show that poststructuralist fictions have not necessarily been any less 'political' than so-called realist novels, and that these were varied responses that often occurred in similar time frameworks, depending on the educational level and affiliations of the writers. A critique of, and debate between "postmodernism" and "postcolonialism" developed as the book unfolded.

As so many aspects of South African life have been hidden and marginalized by the workings of a white racial hegemony and censorship, I wished to discuss more fully works on rural life, especially those by South African women writers. I also wished to demonstrate that rural lives and urban lives have been economically interdependent, with key effects on fictional representation.

I have attempted to make some links between texts that may not have been made before, in terms of writing back to a precursor, the development of a significant literary trope or metaphor, and the dissonances between contemporary reception and reading responses in a post-apartheid context. Family structures and relationships became an important site for understanding political and cultural tensions.

I owe many thanks to colleagues, graduate and undergraduate students over the years for the intellectual stimulus they have provided, especially the graduate students I worked with in Canada at the Institute of Political Economy, Carleton University; at the University of Waterloo, St. Jerome's Collge, which involved a first University of Waterloo graduate course in feminist theory; and at the University of Guelph in a graduate course on South African literature in 1997. The University of Guelph also gave me the opportunity to teach undergraduate and graduate courses in Southern African Literature, as well as Women's Studies.

Ann Clayton

I learned a great deal from conferences organized by the Canadian Association for Commonwealth Languages and Literatures, the MLA conferences I attended, and the intellectual forum created by the Canadian Research Consortium on Southern Africa. Alan Jeeves at Queen's University was a presiding organizer of many of these South African initiatives, as were Dan O'Meara, Miriam Grant, Linda Freeman, John Saul and Rosemary Jolly. Colleagues at Guelph and other Canadian universities have been helpful and generous with insights and suggestions, as well as their critical perspectives. Lindsay Doney was a kind host whil I was a Visiting Professor at the University of Waterloo. Local panels and colloquia on Cultural Studies and Women's Studies added an interdisciplinary dimension to the critiques I developed, as did international conferences in Italy, Germany, and the UK: Bristol, Leeds, and Birmingham. The critical frameworks of Edward Said and Aijaz Ahmad have been an intellectual and moral stimulus to further thought. For links between gender and Southern African politics, I am indebted to the work of Anne McClintock and Linzi Manicom. I am grateful to Jeremy Luke Hill of Vocamus Press, Guelph, for his efficient and professional typesetting and printing services.

Any illuminations these readings of South African novels offer are part of a larger process of radical change which extends much more widely than literature, and is tied to the history of Southern Africa in complex ways. Both fiction and critical responses to fiction are partial attempts to understand, in language and narrative, the historical dimensions of social and individual lives. The chapters that follow are intended to contribute to the ongoing dialogue we call literary criticism. They are also intended to be part of the empowerment of a long-oppressed majority within South Africa, as well as a tribute to the writers and their work, and the courage and perserverance of the African community in South Africa, who finally entered an enfranchised nation in 1994.

Ann Clayton, Guelph, 2017

Chapter One
Citizens and Subjects, Country and Town

Recent debates on postcolonialism, history and literature have emphasized the centrality of narrative processes in the constitution of meaning. Historical and fictional discourses have a "common aspect as semiological apparatuses that produce meanings" (H. White 1987: 1). Narrative is typically concerned with authority and legitimacy, the conflict between desire and law, and is a meta-code "on the basis of which transcultural messages about the nature of a shared reality can be transmitted" (H. White 1987: 1). Recent postcolonial critiques, influenced by poststructuralism and a reinvigorated Marxism, have emphasized the complex relationship between history, narrative, and domination, rather than the original writing back model proposed in *The Empire Writes Back* (Schulze-Engler 1998).[1] There has been a resistance to any monolithic view of colonial domination, and a reading of history as multi-causal and embedded in specific conflicts between historical actors (Ahmad: 1992; Posel 1991). History and temporality are the crucial sites of a struggle for control and legitimacy, but there is no easy access to precolonial cultures or the culture of the colonized (Spivak 1988: 211-213).

As historiography was part of the legitimating apparatus of imperialism, with European history being equated with civilization, fictional narratives have often contested the assumptions of hegemonic historical narratives while being multiply conditioned by their own historical moment. Postcolonial critics thus need to attend to "the hybridized way in which all cultures develop", to the relationship between ideology and literature, and to the different ways in which narratives reconstruct history in order "to uncover a different version of the same history" (Ashcroft 1996: 197). The cultural realm is not autonomous, as colonial expansion was the linchpin of the European transition to capitalism (Loomba 1998: 4). While the colonial discourse studies initiated by Edward Said's *Orientalism* (1978) emphasized ideology, subjectivity and language, there has not been sufficient attention to the interlocking influence of colonialism, capitalism, particular state formations, gender and race on literary production. European colonialism was not monolithic but refracted through different local contexts, intersecting with existing ideologies, practices and hierarchies. Nor is there any single understanding or explanation of decolonization. Patterns of decolonization in Africa, for instance, have made it clear that the historical transition to political independence cannot simply be equated with decolonization: "the dismantling of colonial rule did not automatically bring about changes for the better in the status of women, the working class or the peasantry in most colonized countries" (Loomba 1998: 11-12). Postcolonial critiques thus need to read economics and culture as mutually constitutive domains.

In the South African case, despite the apparently decisive postcolonial moment of 1994, with the first democratic election in which the black majority participated equally, there have been different readings of the nature of colonial rule, and the relationship between nationalism, state formations, resistance and decolonization. Mahmood Mamdani has argued that South Africa is not exceptional to Africa but prototypical, and that the relationship between deracialization and democratization has been asymmetrical in Africa (Mamdani 1996). There has been a division between citizen and subject in all colonial societies, but in Africa debates have turned on liberal solutions, which locate politics in civil society, or communitarian solutions, which put Africa's age-old communities at the center of African politics (Mamdani 1996: 3). In discussing the organization of power in African states, Mamdani refers to the strategies of devolution and containerization which separated the subject population into separate containers under a Native authority, said to be the rightful bearer and enforcer of custom and tradition. This politically strategic colonial policy of tribalism in South Africa took the form of segregationist policy or "apartheid" (as it was called after the Nationalist accession to power in 1948), and one of the chief instruments of control became the policy of "Bantustans" or "homelands" of South Africa, a system involving social engineering and the forced relocations of communities. This policy attempted to consolidate tribal filiations and chieftainships in order to keep Africans out of a centralized state while retaining their labour power in the cities. While a democratic state emphasizes the rights of citizens and law-governed behaviour, in South Africa, because of the belatedness of democratization and the nature of totalitarian racialized rule after 1948, the liberation struggle for racial equality and civil society took place between the patriarchal family and the state (Mamdani 14). Mamdani argues that "the exclusion that defined the specificity of civil society under colonial rule was that of race", but the specific nature of power involves understanding how the subject population was incorporated into the arena of colonial power (Mamdani 15)

In South Africa the divisions between citizen and subject have been particularly harsh, both because of the exclusion of Africans from political voice until 1994 and the brutally enforced system of influx control which policed African urbanization and labour migration. This tension between formal state exclusion and labour incorporation of the African majority provides the context for understanding both the nature of political contestation and cultural production. The labour question is a crucial starting point for understanding the workings of power, and in South Africa forms of rural labour, traditionally performed by women as subsistence agriculturalists, migrant labour to cities and mines, at first predominantly male, and the bifurcated modern urban household of masters, madams and servants form the substructures and themes of literature.

In Mamdani's view, then, "colonialism generalized both the conquest state and the administrative chiefship, and in so doing it wrenched both free of traditional restraint" (40). At the time of pending black majority takeover in South Africa, a novel like Gordimer's *July's People* (1981) reveals how these contesting forms of authority work in practice, in the crucible of totalitarian state control, depleted rural reserves, and the vestiges of traditional African authority. William Beinart's study of contemporary South Africa and its historical formation stresses the social legacies of British imperial presence, and the way in which European capital made the mining industry the economic motor of the country, but points out that in the early twentieth century " a single state was formed but not a single nation" (Beinart 1994: 4). He also stresses the roots of resistance in rural areas: "It was the capacity of black peasants and workers to adapt, increase demographically, educate themselves and strike back politically that has been at the heart of twentieth century South African history"(Beinart 1994: 6).

Colonial and settler intrusion did not simply create new classes, because "westernized" Africans developed their own ideas about the colonial state and their own rights within it (23). Educated Africans sometimes hoped that loyalty to the British Empire would protect them from land-hungry settlers, and challenged settler ideas in their journalism, translations and original literature (23-24). In South Africa the longevity of the migrant labour system has been an overdetermining factor, and Deborah Posel uses the influx control system as a lever to understand the construction and implementation of the apartheid state as a whole. The prevalence of the migrant labour system has an economic explanation: mining capital needed cheap black labour. The costs of social security and labour reproduction were met by the rural reserves, and the mining compound system of single-sex hostels and cheap food gave capitalists a workforce without the cost of supporting workers in town. It was also in capitalist interests for women and children to stay in the reserves (Beinart 28-29). The division of African families thus had its roots in capitalism and the collaboration of ethnic Afrikaner nationalist policy with the needs of mining capital. The nation was defined by these terms of racial exclusivity and labour incorporation, resting on the compatible needs of European controlled mining interests and the white settler state: "State power in South Africa came to be dominated by a group of whites who used the term 'nation' narrowly to mean an ethnically defined segment of about 12% of the population" (Beinart 134). There was "a symbiotic relationship between the mining industry and the state" (Yudelman in Beinart 81) which tended to be masked by English settler liberalism and also by apparent conflict between Afrikaner nationalism and European mining capital interests.

Capitalist land use, argues Beinart, also "entrenched a sharper division in the functions of land than had been the case in pre-colonial society" (50). Though the key pattern of white colonization was the subordination of African farm tenants, which is why the South African farm has operated as such a lasting microcosmic metaphor in fiction, Africans retained some access to land even after the 1913 Land Act, especially as tenant farmers. There were forms of tenacious peasantry in the rural reserves, and migrant labour could be seen as a way for Africans to keep a stake in the rural areas and build up family lineages and ownership. The origins of mass migrancy lay partly in the dynamics of African societies themselves: "by fighting to maintain reserves, rural Africans did not generally accept the terms of segregation as laid down in the 1913 Natives Land Act, nor their exclusion from other rights in society" (Beinar 34). An understanding that rights to land ownership and political participation were closely related plays a part in the phases of resistance in South Africa and those of fictional representation. It also explains why stories of migration and peasant resistance have played such an important role in South African fiction until very recently, with J. M. Coetzee's *Life and Times of Michael K* (1983) and Lauretta Ngcobo's *And They Didn't Die* (1990) being two of the most recent examples.

Conceptualizations of the state in relation to colonialism and decolonization have recently stressed the need to integrate gender perspectives. Linzi Manicom has argued that "the development of apartheid was predicated on state-enforced gender subordination" and fundamental categories of state and politics were constructed and reproduced as masculine categories (444). Manicom argues that "state control and coercion of women was understood as an aspect of the structuring of the system of migrant labour "in early "women's history", and women's struggles were seen as part of their naturalized functions as mothers and wives, or as primarily due to precapitalist African traditions (Bozzoli 1983). Manicom's thesis is that state formation was a gendered and gendering process, and that many earlier analyses have uncritically adopted a patriarchal separation of women's lives into domestic and public spheres, or used a universalizing category of the colonized as male. Gender should not be subordinated to race and class; these social divisions should be shown in complex interaction and as mutually constitutive (Manicom 452). In the historical construction of the colonial state and the policing of migrant labour in South Africa gender ideologies played legitimating roles, categorizing women into "whores" and "unruly women" in the phase of early urbanization (453).

These categories also reproduced the terms of mission Christianity and British imperialism. State policies have thus often reproduced normative gender meanings and subordinate political identities in the same process (456). Joan Scott has pointed out that gender is a "primary field within which or by means of which power is articulated" (Scott 45). Gender meanings are mobilized as metaphors of domination and subordination in relation to specific historical regimes, as they have been by British imperialism, Afrikaner nationalism, and African resistance (Manicom 458-9). Just as some readings of government commissions and their racial exclusions have been gender-blind and have universalized the abstract male African into the central political subject (Ashforth 1990), so more account needs to be taken of the exclusion of white women from the franchise and political citizenship before 1930. Both African and white settler literature before 1930 take on richer meanings when this gender context is seen as crucial rather than marginal, and is read in relation to land, labour and class structures.

In this study I have selected certain crucial historical phases of South African history in order to read a few novels comparatively: the phase of industrialization from 1880 to 1930; the post-war period leading up to the 1948 accession of the Afrikaner Nationalist Party; the 1976 student resistance and township uprisings, and the transition to majority rule in the eighties and nineties. In the comparative readings I have followed through certain historically significant themes in order to show how conservative and progressive ideologies were in tension in these works. "Postcolonial" as a descriptive term "refers to a process of disengagement from the whole colonial syndrome" (Hulme 120). Postcolonial theory has stressed the Gramscian notion of hegemony, and that "subjectivity and ideology are absolutely central to the processes of domination" (Loomba 31). Althusserian notions of ideology discuss both ideological and repressive state apparatuses, and suggest the interpellation of colonial subjects by literature. Terry Eagleton argues in *Criticism and Ideology* that "the linguistic is always at base the politico-linguistic, a sphere within which the struggles of imperial conqueror with subjugated state, nation-state with nation-state, region with nation, class with class are fought out" (54-55). He sees literature as an agent and effect of such struggles, and a zone in which such struggles achieve stabilization (55).

As I have devoted some space to the nexus of events and texts around the Nationalist moment of 1948, his argument is very relevant here: "The moment of consolidation of the nation-state is of paradigmatic significance here – a moment in which the hegemony of a 'national' class reflects itself in the linguistic coherence essential to its integrative, centralizing state apparatuses. The history of the genesis of English as a 'national' language is the history of imperialism and its aftermath..." (55) In South Africa the hegemony of English was contested by the development of Afrikaans, especially after the Anglo-Boer War (1899-1902), the formation of Union in 1910, and the installation of Afrikaans as an equal language in 1925. Bilingualism was introduced into the civil service to promote the interests of Afrikaans-speakers, and thus became an important component of white minority rule, especially as the role of the bureaucracy intensified in the implementation of a myriad apartheid policies. The attempt to enforce Afrikaans as a language of instruction in black township schools was the main catalyst of the 1976 insurrections, indicating the extent to which language policy had become an instrument of political domination and was identified with Afrikaner state power.

Recent postcolonial critiques also stress a need to re-examine the realms between culture or ideology and economics or material reality (Loomba 24). Though ideologies are not always false consciousness they are still produced by economic and social life (Loomba 27). Foucault's work suggests that domination and resistance are linked, and that power works in capillary fashion in daily life (Loomba 51). Literary texts are crucial because they work imaginatively, but they embody ideology in contradictory ways. The Marxist model of the relations of production relies on the idea of the free labourer selling his labour power, but, as Rex has pointed out in South Africa "capitalism was installed through the enforced labour of the Bantu peoples. Thus race relations were crucial in making available a labour force" (Rex 1980; Loomba 125) . In founding South African texts such as Olive Schreiner's novels and stories the coercion of farm labour is a compelling theme. The idea of certain races being suited to particular tasks would be continued in urban areas in job reservation for whites, a lack of skills training for Africans, and the inferior education of Africans for manual labour. For the black working class "race is the modality in which class is lived" (Loomba 133). In representations of colonial life the European is often individuated, while the colonized are represented as plural and anonymous (Hall et al 394).

Postcolonial criticism in a South African context has to take account of the fundamental shift in political history signalled by the first democratic elections in April 1994, while reading that moment against the outlined history of a "racially inscribed capitalism" (Murray 1994: 2). Martin Murray's study of the South African transition to democracy, which is situated within other studies of South African modernization, takes three dialectical pairs of terms to provide an interpretive framework: "continuity and change; organization and spontaneity; and surface appearances and structural underpinnings" (viii) . He stresses a fluid mix of conflict and accommodation, a legacy of embedded structural continuities, and the continuance of vast economic disparities and crystallized class power and privilege. He sees the bargain struck by a white oligarchy as a trading of exclusive political power for continued economic advantage (4). New forms of citizenship for the majority have to be set against these intractable legacies. The movement from confrontation to dialogue is set against the long-term violence and destabilization caused by land appropriation, apartheid rule, the divisiveness of homeland policy, influx control and the mining compound system.

Fiction produced in the eighties and nineties has to be situated within this shifting political landscape and the apartheid legacy. The eighties also saw the construction of broad nonracial associations and civil society. Murray sees these popular movements, democracy from below, as originating in the post-1976 clampdown that eviscerated Black Consciousness organizations (168). The community developments within townships popularized the idea of "non-partisan popular organizations" representing the interests of ordinary people (168). The 'resistance' fiction arising out of the seventies rebellions played a role in creating new "popular subjects" with a collective identity and oriented toward an "alternative popular project" (Touraine 1988). The transition to democracy laid down new faultlines of social conflict, and put pressure on political élites and returned exiles to arrive at workable solutions to political and constitutional crisis (Murray 8-9). The return of exiles after the unbanning of the African National Congress, the Pan-Africanist Congress and the South African Communist Party in 1990 had also played a role in demystifying the liberation movement. This recasting of political alliances and movement from resistance to reconstruction, intermixed with the deep-seated symptoms of the apartheid past, make up the fictional world of Gordimer's *None to Accompany* Me (1994). Postcolonial theory and criticism of South African literature thus have to take account of the slow movement toward democratic rule, the multilayered state which grew out of an imperial past and original colonization, the mechanisms used to implement white minority rule, the moments of crisis and processes of reform constructed to manage crisis along with a degree of autonomy for security forces that often amounted to a police state, and the complex relationship between subjects excluded from citizenship while being conscripted into forms of productive and reproductive labour in country and city. The tension between rural and urban areas, in particular, and the movement of South Africans between them, provides an enduring grid for socio-politically informed critiques of South African literature.

Chapter Two
Rereading South African Culture in the Post-Colony

In South Africa, as Njabulo Ndebele has pointed out, the control of mythology and media has been in the hands of a privileged white minority to whom privilege became second nature (1994: 77). White South Africans have tended to function both as the main producers of literary culture and its analysts, doubly obscuring the agency of black South African writers and intellectuals. Literary criticism has to some degree reproduced the racial ordering of the state, thus tending to discuss literature in "terms that fix culturally defined differences into transcendent "natural " categories or essences" (Gates 1986). As Gates has argued, "race has become a code through which to mystify various forms of economic oppression." (Landry 185). This study hopes to restore some of the ways in which race, gender and material oppression are articulated in narrative representation. This task seems particularly important if we accept the premise of Aijaz Ahmad that "imperialism has won the war against socialism" and therefore "how we pose questions of colony and empire depends on the history of materialities" (1993: 35). In South African cultural critique, issues of race, ethnicity and competing nationalisms have been foregrounded, and the intersections of gender and capitalism with race in both the colonial period and the process of decolonization have been underplayed. In the often comparative critical readings that I offer, I have attempted to show the reciprocal influences and narrative tensions between such multiple determinants.

Traditionally, the South African novel has been read against the history of the rise and fall of racial segregation and the policies that were implemented as part of colonialism and the racialized form it assumed in South Africa, known as apartheid. This has led to views of the novel that stressed a Manichean division into binary racial categories (JanMohamed, Wade).[1] The choice of novels for discussion often suffered from the biases and exclusions of Eurocentric norms.[2] The production of white English-speaking South African novelists has generally been read as an expression of liberal humanism, and 'black' fiction as the vehicle of socio-political protest (Rich 1982; Ndebele 1989; 1994). Some critics, especially diasporic African critics, have reacted to black South African fiction very dismissively, as in Lewis Nkosi's 1965 opinion that "it is impossible to detect in the fiction of black South Africans any significant and complex talent which responds with both vigour of the imagination and sufficient technical resources to the problems posed by conditions in South Africa" (1965: 21). Neither Sol T. Plaatje nor Peter Abrahams seemed to deserve much detailed critical attention, and their critical study was left mainly to academic recuperative research projects which tended to emphasize sociological context over critical analysis, or linkage with other texts. Moreover, Nkosi's view, which homogenized "protest fiction" as superficially organized around slogans and symbols, was reiterated by Njabulo Ndebele in a few articulate and influential essays that separated politics and aesthetics into distinct realms: "literature (by black South Africans) has located itself in the field of politics.... without discovering and defining the basis of its integrity as an art form" (1994: 86). I have set out to show that there are differences between so-called 'protest' novels, and also to highlight the interconnections of race, gender and class as they are played out in a few of these narratives.

Stephen Gray's *Southern African Literature: An Introduction* which appeared in 1979, questioned earlier surveys of the novel, periodized literary production, and replaced any posited unity with the metaphor of a literary archipelago linked by conscious and unconscious myths. He pointed out that Ezekiel Mphahlele's *The African Image* (1962) had begun a classification of South African literature as part of African literature in English. This critical tradition has not really been extended, except in discussion of the oral tradition, but the current moment might be a useful one in which to view South African fiction in the context of the cultural analysis proposed by African writers and critics such as Ngugi wa Th'iongo and Chinua Achebe, who have emphasized the embeddedness of language and convention in European colonial discourse, and the need for a decolonized critical consciousness. Peter Abrahams's *A Wreath for Udomo* (1956) is an important but neglected forerunner for West African novels of post-independence struggles, forms of neocapitalist corruption, and national leadership. Florence Stratton's recent study of African fiction offers a stimulating model for reading African novelists in intertextual dialogue, and for reading male and female novelists in the context of recent innovative debates about gender politics.

Gray's critical study of Southern African literature examines the white man's creation myths in Southern Africa, frontier myths, the imaginary voyage, the rise and fall of the colonial hunter, Olive Schreiner and the novel tradition, and the emergence of "black English". The lack of gender analysis in his delineation of foundational myth has been questioned by Dorothy Driver, who has shown how mythic readings are themselves implicated in gendered perceptions and patriarchal structures of thought (Driver 1992). Gray takes Olive Schreiner's novel, *The Story of an African Farm* (1883) as the fountainhead of a liberal realist tradition. This tradition, he argues, parodied colonial adventure fiction and its heroes, took self-education as its theme, began the South African figuration of a wandering 'meester ' or teacher/interloper, a feminized frontiersman, and an aspiring, thwarted feminist, and established the alienation of the white South African colonizer from a stultifying landscape. He sees the static and death-driven fatalism of Schreiner's world as continuing through other novelists who could be described as her heirs: Pauline Smith, William Plomer, Alan Paton, Dan Jacobson and Nadine Gordimer.

In his final chapter on the emergence of black South African writing and its intersections with an older oral tradition, Gray calls for a "revised, broadened poetics" (168) and mentions that "hybridization is a natural and normal part of literary fermentation" (166). Written and oral literatures, he argues, are interdependent. An interpretation or reclassification of Schreiner's novel has often been the starting point of a revisioning of the South African novel in English. Tony Voss's 1977 analysis of the pastoral mode as central and recurrent in South African fiction also began with a genre classification of Schreiner's *The Story of an African Farm*, and was followed by further genre classifications of the South African novel into Romance, Pastoral, Realism and Fabulation (Voss 1977; Christie at al., 1980). Recent critical readings of Schreiner's novel have positioned her within an emancipatory strand of modernism and as a critic of the collusive workings of capitalism, patriarchy and colonialism, rather than a founding representative of white settler alienation in Africa (Berkman, Clayton, Gorak, Monsman).

South African fiction can be usefully located within current debates on postcolonial identities in Africa, which seek to keep historical and political analysis central while allowing that the idea of a plurality of spheres "prevents the story of ethnic difference in Africa" from overwhelming larger debates (Werbner 1996: 1). Earlier linear models of postcolonialism have given way to a debate on ideas of historical rupture at independence versus continuity of the structures of power. I have sought to keep the idea of cultural process and struggle alive in the analysis of selected novels, in order to show how identity is reconstituted in narratives which depict the heritage of different forms of interlocking oppression. Specific policies have denaturalized the black South African's identity from birth, and made the white South African a part of the problem of fictional self-representation. Richard Werbner has suggested that postcolonial studies must foreground the state and state-created domains for a number of reasons, including the transformation of the state, the importance of political violence, reciprocal assimilation of elites, political hybridity and stereotyping (7). The role of political violence has been crucial in South Africa, and looms large in narrative representation. Aijaz Ahmad offers a summary of the features that have made South Africa an example of "recalcitrant settler colonialism": a consolidated class of African proletariat; the alliance between the ANC and the Communist Party; the expansion of ANC hegemony and the favourable climate created by the emancipation of the Portuguese colonies.

Within postcolonial theory, the concepts developed by Homi Bhabha to describe minority and migrant spaces and narrative temporality are relevant here. The "social articulation of difference," he argues, "is a complex, on-going negotiation that seeks to authorize cultural hybridities that emerge in moments of historical transformation" (Bhabha 1994: 1). This study plans to look comparatively at a few of these moments of historical transformation in South Africa to see how fictional narratives at the time negotiate singular and communal "strategies of selfhood" (Bhabha 1994: 1) . Narrative representations of competing communities produce the terms of cultural engagement, seek to change them, and negotiate cultural value.

Such concepts of cultural hybridity are germane to a critical re-visioning of the South African novel, as they question the ideas of linear enlightenment invoked by the "post" in postapartheid, postfeminism, and postcolonialism (see McClintock 1992; 1995: 9-17). Instead of looking to the novel as a transmitter of an unquestioned national culture or the product of a determinate racial divide, critics can then look across cultures, ethnicities, and communities, the public and private spheres, as these are reproduced within fictional narratives at specific historical conjunctures. The cultural life of the nation is then seen as unconsciously lived, an approach that Stephen Clingman has used more specifically in applying the theories of Frederic Jameson on the political unconscious to the novels of Nadine Gordimer (1986). This approach is particularly suited to South Africa, where the legislated racial inequalities of society have produced intense unconscious processes of projection and abjection, and also specific themes and tropes within the South African novel, such as miscegenation, racial crime and punishment', madness, violence, infanticide, murder, and ideas of taint and degeneration connected with inter-racial contact.

Fiction in South Africa has been powerfully concerned to represent processes of displacement, those processes that are now seen as a defining condition of postcolonial sensibility and migrancy after globalization. Yet these processes were also a literal effect of apartheid legislation, the influx control that monitored urbanization and mining labour and the forced removals that attempted to retribalize the communities originally displaced by land theft, political exclusion and industrialization.

The idea of hybridity as a form of cultural interdependence, "the creation of new transcultural forms within the contact zone produced by colonization " (Ashcroft et al., 1996: 118) is relevant to a cross-cultural and cross-racial imaginary in Southern Africa.[3] Revisionist history in South Africa has been a stimulus to reading Southern Africa in terms of gradual intercultural adaptation across various boundaries. Recent historians have stressed the gradual cultural osmosis and transfer that occurred between communities and ethnicities on the frontier, between Khoi and San, hunter and pastoral bands, Khoisan and Bantu farmers, Boer and Brit (Bundy, Elphick, Guy). Thus a picture emerges of more continuity and commonality, both in the foundational phases of Southern African settlement and in the succeeding phases, where literature could symbolically anticipate future forms of multi-racial collaboration to set against the confrontations that occurred under segregationist law.

This context can be used to frame early forms of African literacy such as Plaatje's *Mhudi*. It also enables the South African novel in English to be seen as a site of contesting forms of language, orality and literacy, inter-communal contact and communication. There are cross-cultural affiliations, local adaptations of the novel genre and of European tropes to re-represent imperial culture, while questioning the relevance of its values and norms to Southern Africa.[4] In this respect, South African fiction can be read as one instance of postcolonial fiction, which is "an instrument of and a commentary on political and cultural independence" (May 269). I have tried to show how different novels legitimate or subvert racist mythology, in that clusters of myths have played a powerful role in legitimating South African racial segregation (Thompson 1985).

Many feminist critics have suggested that gender has been a neglected dimension of the revolutionary dynamic in South Africa, but also of the critical analysis of cultural production (Bradford, Walker). Earlier critics of postcolonial fiction also tended to assume that in South Africa race replaced class (JanMohamed). More recently, as in Gwen Bergner's work on Fanon, it has seemed important to show how sexuality and language are inflected by race, to delineate "the interdependence of race and gender" (1995: 77), and to demonstrate that "the traffic in women not only describes an economy of heterosexuality but also marks a conjunction of the sexual economy with the material economy" (1995: 81). Anne McClintock has outlined, in her searching analysis of the workings of western imperialism in Southern Africa, many of the concepts that I have utilized in literary analysis. She suggests that underlying industrial modernity lies the conquest of the sexual and labour power of colonized women, but that there are also alternative female powers and "alternative African notions of time and knowledge" (1995: 3). White Englishmen gave birth to three orders: "the male, reproductive order of patriarchal monogamy; the white economic order of mining capital; and the global political order of empire" (4). These interlinked concepts are relevant to the analysis of the South African settler novel, which dwells from the outset on the single mother and the illegitimate child as the signs of gender predicaments and feminist resistance, and which creates linkages between female sexuality, urbanization, mining labour and capital. McClintock sees the cult of domesticity as a crucial dimension of male and female identity and an element of the imperial enterprise.

Feminists who have outlined the relationship between private and public spheres in women's oppression have also suggested the complexity of these uneven relationships that complicate race, class and gender (Bozzoli 1983). Gender dynamics secure imperial power, and the colour critique of feminism has made it clear how collusive white South African women have been in structures of privilege and power. A number of critics have argued for a close relationship between materialist notions of history, culture and subjectivity (Delphy 1984; Kuhn and Wolpe 1978; Landry and MacLean 1993; Hennessy 1993). This emphasis is especially useful in the analysis of fiction, where notions of family and sexuality are crucial, and are mediated by the broader workings of class, racially ordered capitalism, and colonialism. Domestic space in South Africa has always been racialized through the complicated workings of the employer / servant dynamic, which has material and psychoanalytic dimensions. One of the key concepts here has been Julia Kristeva's concept of abjection, a process whereby social beings are constituted through the expulsion of elements society deems impure; these expelled elements then haunt the edges of the subject's identity (Kristeva 1982). Kristeva's model has a great deal of explanatory power for South African fiction, with its fraught racially tense relationships in which illegitimate desire and abjection contend for mastery. The concepts of abjection, expulsion and haunting are useful in analyzing the fiction of "miscegenation' in South Africa, employer/servant relationships in the novel, and the processes of confrontation that the South African novel often orchestrates in order to lay bare the inner dynamic of a racially ordered society.

Further concepts that McClintock discusses are cross-dressing and fetishism as they complicate and question imperial and narrative authority. Schreiner's foundational novel draws on both of these psychoanalytically suggestive processes in *The Story of an African Farm*, in which a young English settler cross-dresses to become a nurse, and a young woman's muslin dresses and tiny feet become the fetishes of colonial femininity. These contradictory processes do tend to suggest that women's doubleness under patriarchy is unavoidable, as Juliet Mitchell has argued (Mitchell 1975), but recent feminists have been concerned to discover what grounds there are for a theory of gender power and agency. Some feminists have argued that the Lacanian model inscribes women permanently as objects in the order of exchange. Women are then constantly reproduced as subordinate, but feminist critics need to ask how fiction can represent and endorse strategies for change and empowerment. "Materialist feminist history" argues Rosemary Hennessy, acknowledges that its readings are historical and provisional, but must labour to release "the unsaid of feminist praxis", and thus "strengthen the oppositional power of feminism's collective subject and emancipatory aims" (1993: 138).

Feminist psychoanalytic theory, which suggests that the fetish embodies "castration or its denial" (McClintock 1995: 201), might prove useful, for example, in the analysis of Bessie Head's *The Collector of Treasures* story sequence, in which the castration of African men symbolizes both the intensely destructive effects of colonialism, capitalism, and racism with African patriarchy, and women's outrage against their disadvantages within these systems.[5] In *The Story of an African Farm* the figure of the transvestite is one which disrupts the gender binaries operative in colonial society (Garber 1992). In Doris Lessing's *The Grass is Singing* the whip is a fetishistic signal of both colonial and racial domination, while the fact that it is seized and used by a woman, Mary Turner, signals an inversion of traditional gender authority within the colony and highlights the relationship between racial power and colonial marriage. Forms of agency and resistance can be located within figural representation and within women's roles as the producers of new cultural meanings in fiction. As Ashcroft has argued: "If the power of discourse over the subject can be represented by writing then the capacity of the subject to write itself into being, by an interpolation into the grand narrative of history, becomes a primary mode of postcolonial agency" (1996: 199).

A further question that McClintock asks is how "nationalism is implicated in gender power" (1995: 353). This question relates to how South African fiction at different historical moments has displayed notions of agency, citizenship, family roles and sexual identity. Women have typically been constructed as icons of nationhood while being relatively powerless as citizens and political beings (Boehmer; Kandiyoti). If the family became "both the organizing figure for national history and its antithesis" (McClintock 357), the constructions of families in fiction become politically significant, from the orphans and changelings of Schreiner's fictions to the rural African family that Lauretta Ngcobo uses as a figure of resistance. Migrant labour has created so many familial divisions and shuttlings between homelands and urban spaces in South Africa, and the racial hierarchy of the urban South African family has had so many devastating social and political implications, that representations of the family in South African fiction are packed with allegorical signification for the wider political order.

Questions of land inheritance, children, and marriage are tied to the family structures and negotiations that often make up the plots of novelistic narrative. At the same time, there is no single narrative of the nation, and it is the business of criticism to explore differences between fictional relationships of family to nation, and suggest their political meanings. Which people or groups of people have been expelled, abjected, fantasized or incorporated into the family in fictional narratives at different times remains a core question. Fanon has argued that "the dynamics of colonial power are fundamentally though not solely, the dynamics of gender" (McClintock 1995: 364), though the homosocial dynamic of Fanonist paradigms again excludes the presence of black women as cultural actors (Bergner).

South African historian Jeff Guy has described African women's labour as being the fulcrum about which the phases of colonial power have turned, and which the later sex-gender system consolidated (Guy 1990). A feminist critique then needs to examine how representations of labour, domestic space, sexuality and citizenship function within the South African novel to consolidate or subvert white settler dominance and a wider order of capitalist hegemony. Ideologies of motherhood and the politics of sexuality have carried different meanings at different historical moments and have depended on the subjectivity of the writers concerned, and the shifting responses of their readers, as well as differentiated European and African norms (Walker 1998).[6]

In the following comparative critical discussions of selected South African novels, these paradigms of genre adaptation, cultural transfer and osmosis, family and national structures, race, class, and gender, will be utilized to explore how progressive or emancipatory particular narratives were at the moment of origin, judged in the retrospective light of the struggle toward a non-racial democracy. Which forms of power were consolidated, and whose interests were served by the pattern and bias of representation? These critical questions may enable readings of the South African novel which serve the emergent interests and voices of those who have traditionally been voiceless, not only in politics, but also in the novel that has carried the burden of competing narratives at any given time. This is important in South Africa, where the structures of racial segregation and dispossession still exert a compelling force, so that South Africa challenges any "simple notions of post-colonial literatures in English" (Walder 154).

Cultural analysis, Stephen Greenblatt has argued, depends on scrupulous formal analysis, and is never extrinsic. Novels, like other literary works, set up both forms of constraint and forms of mobility. This policing of cultural boundaries has been particularly important in South African literature, which has often internalized a set of hegemonic racial policies and taboos, as well as testing the forms and limits of transgression that those segregationist policies have invited. Greenblatt sets out a series of questions around culture and literature, such as which models of practice a text enforces; why certain models are compelling at a given time; how the values of the text interact with a reader's values; what social understanding is implied; what freedoms are constrained, and how larger social structures are connected with critical evaluations.

In the development of South African literature these questions are crucial, given that in South Africa extremely constraining racial policies, forms of labour control, land domination by a white minority, and brutal police enforcement of state policies have been the norm, and effected a highly racialized form of colonial rule until as late as 1990. The ways in which characters engage in and negotiate the boundaries of their culture thus become crucial to an understanding of the novel, and also of the interplay between protagonists, antagonists, and witnesses that constructs the epistemological basis of a new understanding within narrative. It seems as though the state itself, with its massive legislative machinery and law enforcers, often forms the antagonist in South African fiction. "Novels thematize their own place in culture" (229), suggests Greenblatt, but even the status of liberal classics like Alan Paton's *Cry, the Beloved Country* (1948) has been interrogated at different points of South African history, both because of the different historical phases of repression and resistance, and the very different social locations of critics within South Africa's highly stratified and unequal society.

Once one reads a culture as a network of negotiations for the exchange of goods, ideas and people (through enslavement, adoption, and marriage, for instance), then the novel can be read as a transmitter of cultural norms which nevertheless often subverts those norms. Close analysis involves an understanding of the ways in which apartheid classification or control has been legitimated at different stages of political absolutism and resistance. The ideas of kinship and prohibition promulgated by anthropologists seem more appropriate to traditional African culture within South Africa, but much of South African literature has recorded the breakdown of traditional kinship systems under the impact of colonial rule, and revealed the patchworks of cultural habits created in homelands, townships and urban slums. Liberal novelists have sometimes drawn on these kinship patterns to contrast with them the patterns of political affiliation created as whites joined in the opposition to apartheid rule.

A key question in the following analyses will thus concern the social and culturally symbolic functions of particular novels as they responded to historical moments and created their memorable characters to walk along the boundaries of constraints and freedoms available at that time. This passage from tradition to modernity has involved a displacement of a mythic mentality and the birth of what

JanMohamed has called a "historical consciousness" in Africa (9).

The shape of South African culture is partly determined by the replacement of an oral culture by a literate one, and this has had many effects on those involved in both traditions, which have been in constant interaction since the arrival of missionary literacy and printing presses in the nineteenth century.[7] Though the first novels by black South Africans were only written in the early twentieth century, they were highly influenced by the European genres and styles that were used as the vehicles of literacy and education. Conversely, white South African novelists, superficially working within the mode of European social realism, have drawn on African myth and ritual as a storehouse of themes, tropes and narrative structures. Some writers, such as Bessie Head, have deliberately constructed their short stories and novels around the mixture of African storytelling modes and Western narrative habits in order to illustrate the complex effects of a Christian colonial culture on pre-literate African village life.

Tracing some of these mutual articulations of orality and literacy, African tradition and Western assumptions through the development of the South African novel may help to suggest hitherto unnoticed forms of commonality and cultural reciprocity, as well as traces of colonial legitimation. Isobel Hofmeyr has outlined the impact of gender on the types of story traditionally told by African men and women, and the locations of their storytelling, with men as the main transmitters of historical, public stories and women the tellers of more intimate domestic tales. This comparative distinction may illuminate the ways in which later novelists like Sipho Sepamla, Mongane Serote, and Miriam Tlali negotiated the crisis of 1976 differently in their fictions, with gender difference as one of the significant variables.[8]

Fiction, according to Hillis Miller, encourages writers and readers to experiment with different selves, South African fiction has fantasized along racial lines to contest the laws of apartheid, and earlier the laws of a patriarchal colonial culture. Connections between racial and gender boundaries are thus especially complex in South African literature. From the time of Olive Schreiner onward dreaming has often been a form of transgression and healing, the creation of a make-believe world in which, as Achebe has suggested, threats to the self can be negotiated (Achebe 1988: 117). Narratives often dramatize an initiation into the harsh realities of frontier culture and later a racially demarcated culture. Novels reveal the core stories of a culture, and in South Africa these have often been of transgression and punishment, fantasized cross-racial encounters both conservatively and rebelliously imaged, the journey from country to city, the stresses of inter-racial contact within cities, and the moral and psychological costs of long maintained white minority rule on both colonizers and colonized.

"Miscegenation" may be one of those complex words or figures described by William Empson as standing at the centre of a narrative (Miller 77), in this case a national narrative South Africa has told itself repeatedly in images of forbidden and fulfilled desire. Such a complex word may be "the crossroads of fundamentally incongruous meanings" (Miller 77). Miscegenation is a socially constructed taboo that has had endless material and cultural consequences in countries like South Africa. It is thus a concept in which biological and cultural factors intersect in a complex way. Both the incest and miscegenation taboos were designed to enforce categories of sexual relations, and women tended to function "as commodities mediating social and symbolic relationships among men" (Bergner 81).[9]

Along with the development of an ethical consciousness of the damages done by separate development and racist laws, there has been a growing sense in white writing of the difficulty of telling stories effectively and morally in a South African environment, especially when a sense of responsibility towards a politically voiceless majority coincided with a developing sensitivity to Western appropriations of indigenous culture. The development of the South African novel in English thus demonstrates partial answers to these aesthetic problems, which are also moral and culturally determined problems.

As postmodernism and postcolonialism tend to be linked in later phases of postcolonial fiction (King 1996: 37), I have tried to illustrate the emergence of forms of self-reflexivity in some novels, and to suggest which interests and angles of political vision they have served. The novel made a late appearance for black South African Writers, and has not been the dominant or perhaps the key mode of expression; usually popular culture, music, autobiography and short fiction are emphasized. The emergence of the novel for black South

Africans can be seen as part of a wider African paradox well described by JanMohamed: "Northrop Frye has argued that it is the link with history and temporal context that has confined the novel as a predominant form to the western world. But now literacy, by destroying the oral cultures in Africa and rendering possible the development of historical consciousness, has made the novel an integral part of the new syncretic African societies" (283).

The novel for black South Africans has been a part of a movement into modernity and a literate culture, but it has also orchestrated a movement into the cities with all its attendant political and cultural meanings. In particular, I have tried to show how the organic movement toward citizenship was thwarted by apartheid rule, and yet the novel itself became one of the cultural weapons to articulate the spirit and activity of resistance to apartheid. As Ten Kortenaar has pointed out with respect to Chinua Achebe's fiction, while colonization has had specific and damaging effects, the construction of narrative offers "possibilities for collective self-definition and action" in which Africans have become "not the victims but the makers of their own history" (1995: 40).

The multilingual mixture in South Africa has made the rendering of different languages and dialects a problem for the South African novelist from the start, and Olive Schreiner writes of the difficulty of rendering Cape Dutch, for instance. Linguistic registers can be used to create particular aesthetic effects; they sometimes mark or mask forms of cultural superiority; they resonate with particular ideologies, such as a biblical typology associated with the Great Trek or with Liberal enlightenment on matters of race (see J. M. Coetzee, 1988). The multilingual composite of South Africa has made such artistic problems central, and has made the theme of communication and miscommunication across cultural and racial boundaries central since Schreiner published *The Story of an African Farm* in 1883. Given the intimate relationships of power, ideology and fiction in South Africa, and the dismantling of aspects of the apartheid order, it seems appropriate to reread the enterprise of fiction in the light of these changes.

What is offered here is not a survey or a comprehensive description of the development of the novel in South Africa. It is rather an attempt to situate a few texts comparatively within the dialectic of complex political and cultural struggles towards democracy. Ndebele has suggested that interpreters have an important role "to promote… the broad social interest to the extent that that interest has been accurately defined" (1994: 84). Though I disagree with Ndebelle's polarization of fiction and popular culture, I agree with his account of the critic's role in such circumstances, "to reveal and restore to the oppressed the history of their cultural practice" (1994: 119). Given the distortions of white consciousness, it also seems to be important to describe what rereading key South African novels in English is like for one white feminist critic at this historical juncture, with the benefit of some historical hindsight, and at a distance. The concept of citizenship has taken on new meaning in South Africa and the development of fiction illuminates its historical construction. These essays are written within a politics of memory, which has to recognize both distance and familiarity, and reconstitute a world in which we are constantly rewritten by culture.

Chapter Three
Gender and Narrative: Olive Schreiner and Pauline Smith

> Lyndall: "'Do you take an interest in the position of women, Waldo?... If I might but be one of those born in the future; then, perhaps, to be born a woman will not be to be born branded.'" – Olive Schreiner, *The Story of an African Farm*

Current debates in postcolonial theory often contest the boundaries of nation itself, and mention "the uneasy relationship between nationalism and liberation" (Said 1993: 63). In recent history the collapse of the Soviet Union and Yugoslavia "suggests that a narrower nationalism readily offers itself as an alternative to personal immersion in the historical dialectic of the totalitarian State" (Hawley xvii). Individuals are seen as having multiple affiliations rather than as being defined by nationhood. The route toward democracy in South Africa has been tortuous, and many aspects of the socialist dream of the 1955 Freedom Charter had to be jettisoned in the politics of negotiation that led to a democratic constitution.

Recent discussions of memory and nation in South Africa have stressed the importance of the relativity of memory (Coetzee and Nuttall). Whose memories are valued as a democratic order and civil society are established? The politics of memory have become crucial as contending ethnic nationalisms debate political structure, the distribution of land and power, and whether or not the healing and reconciliation of individuals image a national process. Literature is one of the crucial sites where memory is created and inscribed, and where the nation is constructed. Rereading South African novels at this juncture can reveal where forms of cultural custodianship have been created, and how ethnicity, race and gender have been constructed at crucial conjunctures of South African history. These readings are at the same time those of a white South African woman living outside the country, with the shift in perspective this implies.

In the struggle toward democracy, there has been an "often unquestioned perpetuation of women's inferior status in emerging nations" (Hawley xiv). In South Africa women have been badly under-represented in political structures, constituting only 3.5% of the lower house, and 2.8% of the upper house in the legislature in 1994 (Klugman). South African history has created vast schisms among women, so that conceptions of feminism have seemed not only different but opposite in direction at certain points. White middle-class feminists, influenced by European and North American feminist consciousness, have conceptualized autonomy in independence from domesticity and family , while many black South African women organized around the slogan of motherhood to protest the separation of families under the migrant labour system (Klugman). During the seventies and eighties the African mother could become a focal point for resistance, especially as class and economic interests clearly made African women the lowest in the hierarchy of privilege. Critics have pointed out that this icon of African motherhood has not necessarily forwarded women's political claims to citizenship, and have sometimes obscured the actual differences in class, ethnicity and economic privilege.

In her discussion of gender in African literature, Florence Stratton argues that women are often identified with static African traditions, or with sexuality (mothers or prostitutes), and in the African novel men take childbirth as a conclusive metaphor for public struggle, while women make the problematic role of mothering a topic (Stratton: 8, 14, 53). McCluskie and Innes write: "The colonizer's mythologizing of Africa as the Other, as recognizably Female... (is) all too often transformed into recognizably related forms by African male writers in the name of nationalism" (quoted by Stratton, 18). Achebe, for instance, is seen as creating a version of the sexual allegory "while seeking to subvert the Manichean allegory of race" (37). The reiterated rhetorical use in black South African literature of the Mother Africa trope and of pregnancy or childbirth as a form of symbolic closure in fiction does indicate, however, how destructive apartheid ideology has been when racial difference has served as the linchpin of policy and economic reward. Representations of motherhood and family structures thus become significant in narratives, revealing and concealing different cultural and national aspirations, and how these may be differently thwarted or promoted for men and women.[1]

Contemporary feminism also stresses the reciprocal construction of masculinity as a focus of feminist critique. South African society, with its traditionally polarized codes of masculinity and femininity, has influenced the representation of both sexes within fiction. Novels have also deconstructed those classifications from the outset. Contrary narrative directions, inversion of gender stereotypes, and conflicting ideological trajectories in the representation of indigenous peoples, are certainly features of Olive Schreiner's *The Story of an African Farm* (1883). In this sense the recent phenomenon of "gay fiction" represents a further, much more sexually explicit, development of a gender deconstruction begun by Schreiner (Heyns).

In 1862, the year that Lyndall and Em (the young female protagonists of the novel) are twelve years old, Em says plaintively: "I suppose some day we shall go somewhere; but now we are only twelve, and we cannot marry till we are seventeen. Four years, five, that is a long time to wait. And we might not have diamonds if we did marry" (38). Marriage sets the boundary of Em's expectation at this point, and education is Lyndall's goal, partly because she perceives she is out of the line of land inheritance, and the farm will go to Em. Nevertheless, her aims are also wealth and a ladylike refinement that will put Tant Sannie, the 'Boer-woman', to shame. Schreiner thus sketches in the role expectations of women at mid-century: the fashionable magazines that come from Europe and are pinned up in colonial farmhouses; the relation of land inheritance to white settler marriage, and women's aspiration toward education in the latter half of the nineteenth century. Lyndall's comparison of the drops on an "ice plant" with the real diamonds she covets establishes the figure of mineral wealth that was about to transform the face of South Africa in the rush towards the Kimberley diamond fields, and the revolutions in transport, labour, and industrialization that would shortly follow. Em's words also indicate that mobility was determined by their sex and marital status, that in colonial society at the time girls often married young, and that land acquisition and consolidation were major motives in marriage. This point is expanded in the portrayal of Tant Sannie's next marriage, and in the ambitious manoeuvres of the European interloper, Bonaparte Blenkins.

Blenkins serves as a compendium figure of Europe in Southern Africa at a time when the frontier was closing, when economic and social encroachment were intensifying before the industrial revolution: " I... have been in every country in the world and speak every civilized language, excepting only Dutch and German" (52). He also represents in parodic form the motives of European economic intervention in Africa, the idea of European cultural supremacy, and the nature of the actual pact that would follow between European capital and South African mineral wealth: "I had money, I had lands, I said to my wife, 'There is Africa, a struggling country; they want capital; they want men of talent; they want men of ability to open up that land. Let us go'" (54).

Blenkins runs the gamut of colonial roles available at the time to a European opportunist: beggar, phoney schoolmaster at the farm, phoney preacher, suitor to a Dutch farm-owner, overseer of the farm, suitor to a younger and richer niece, fugitive, and finally the husband of another widowed Dutch landowner. Marriage, and not the development of local talent and imagination that young Waldo's sheep-shearing machine represents, is his route to wealth and success in the Cape Colony. The highly satiric representation of Blenkins displays the allegiances of a first generation South African novelist who makes the links between economic and sexual exploitation, yet sees in such Boer-Brit alliances the closing of an economic pact that crushed the Christian enlightenment of the gullible missionary, Old Otto, and perceived liberal sentiment and education of the native as spurious. When the missionary Otto says of Tant Sannie's Khoi (Hottentot) servant: "'Virtuous!' said the German; "I have confidence in her. There is that in her which is pure, that which is noble' " (76-77), he is being satirized for his belief in the noble savage, but he is also outlining the social, even revolutionary implications of the missionary creed, that men and women are born equal, and are capable of nobility despite skin colour: "They [the missionaries] stamped science on nature; and on history, revolution" (Elphick 1988: 278). Thus the polarization that occurred around the issue of slave emancipation in 1838, and the hostilities between Boer and missionary camps that triggered the Great Trek are dramatized in *African Farm* in character conflict. At the level of narrative tone and point-of-view, however, British cultural supremacy is reaffirmed in the denigration of the coarse-featured Em, and in the racially stereotyped and degraded "Hottentots" and "Kaffirs", satirized for having aspirations towards European dress and civilization and for being sycophantic mimics and dependents of the Cape Dutch rural order. A whole set of uneasy sentiments around racial, ethnic and cultural hierarchy and denigration is set in play within the text, with humour as a partial solvent for brutality and exploitation of many kinds.

The Story of an African Farm, written in the 1870s, is set back in time, and the time of the action is linked to the great drought of 1862, in the aftermath of the Xhosa cattle-killings in 1857 which decimated the Xhosa people and their belief system (Voss 1977). Thus the Africans are depicted as the broken and subservient people they were at the time, though their denigrated physical features are part of the narrative's involvement in British imperialism and an evolutionary model of human development. The development of the plot in terms of the surviving and victimized characters is a satirical and gender-adapted illustration of Darwin's theory of the "survival of the fittest". The farm society in which we see representatives of different cultural communities colliding, misunderstanding one another, seeking ascendancy, is still that of the Southern African frontier zone, "a zone of interaction among peoples practicing different cultures", where "a decisive struggle for political power is taking place" (Elphick 1988: 270).[2]

The attempts made to bring about socio-economic integration on the frontier, chiefly by Sir George Grey (1854 – 1861), have not penetrated to Tant Sannie's domain, where the Xhosa servants are excluded from the Sunday morning church service. Nevertheless, in the second section of the novel the farmhouse, representing the social order and women's consciousness, is a more congenial and compassionate place, where Em's listening skills and patience are enshrined.

By making Lyndall an elfin, beautiful orphan, Schreiner attempts to free her main protagonist from the cultural field within which she operates, but Lyndall also suffers from the closed communities around her, which operate around class, land, and economic interests, and keep forming new alliances. Her venture into finishing school embitters her, and her sexual alliances, which she tries to construct in a free zone, prove disastrous. There are no free zones for sexuality. Her ambition to become an actress is thwarted by pregnancy, and thus the binary of production and reproduction, creativity and biological constraint, is described in Lyndall's life story. The sign of the unmarried mother, illegitimate childbirth and death thus marks a questioning of colonialism, patriarchy and the ownership of resources by these censorious, anti-intellectual and anti-emancipatory interests. The doctrines of separate spheres for women, the angel in the house, marriage as a form of private property, and the ideology of female submission are refracted through a crass frontier culture (see Marcus). "The ideology of imperialism, based on the structure of the patriarchal family, needed woman's consent to dependency and rewarded her with power over her servants" (Marcus 73). The cultural contrast between Lyndall and Em as English and Anglo-Afrikaner reflects the dual effects of gender ideology and economic interest: Lyndall has ladylike refinement without economic means; Em has domestic talents, will inherit the farm, and is traditionally subservient.

In the Victorian Künstlerroman, of which *The Story of an African Farm* is a colonial example, there is an inevitable contradiction between feminist discourse and biography. Artistic production and biological reproduction are often contradictory models in novels which show the "birth of the artist as heroine" (Gubar). As the careers of the children show, "domesticity competes with the ethos of work as a scheme for ordering life" (Gubar 40). There is a dual artist figure in *African Farm*, with Lyndall aspiring to be an actress and Waldo an untrained sculptor. The narrative moves between different objects of satire, while showing that Lyndall and Waldo inhabit the space of victimization because they have aspirations towards a unity of imagination and intellect, labour and social service. Waldo is the figure of the indigenous artist and keeps alive in the text the memory of earlier waves of settlement and destruction in the San rock artist. He thus attempts to carry the best of indigenous knowledge and art into the scientific age with his invented sheep-shearing machine, and is a martyr to the paradigm shift occurring at the moment of industrialization.

The discourse around stock-theft which leads to the ousting of old Otto and the herdsman, and which marks the earlier frontier phase of South African history, gives way to a fierce competition around land and economic resources, still largely cemented in marital alliances, but on the cusp of the industrial mining of minerals in South Africa.

Though the imaging of land ownership in marriage is farcical, the structure of marriage and the system of land inheritance it fostered is not. Waldo's brutal beating by Blenkins, the death of Lyndall and her child, and Em's compromised marriage are all markers of the European modernity that has invaded the farm, and the censorious Cape Dutch faith that fostered a racist order on the farm in the first place, relegating the indigenous inhabitants to slaves and washers of white feet, a scene replicated a few times in the text. Waldo's beating can be read as a displaced punishment for stock-theft, which does occur in the novel with regard to the herdsman. A harsh beating for stock-theft was a scene that Schreiner had witnessed when growing up, as it was a frequently administered punishment.

Figures like Waldo serve purposes of racial as well as class ideology in early South African fiction; Waldo partly represents the potential and the exploitation of a labouring class. Blenkins's sadistic cruelty to Waldo, who is first described as a herdsman, is also a figure for the rampant opportunism that operated within Southern African society in general at this time of historical struggle. Wanton cruelty, both random and excessive, is the excess which marks this historical period of colonial war and destruction. The closing of the frontier that was ending a sequence of seven frontier wars between the Cape Colony and the Xhosa people is shown to have a gender and racial component, disempowering intelligent women, crippling the scientific genius emerging out of a rejected Calvinist theology, and incorporating a degraded servant class. Elphick has argued that at the closing of the frontier after military sovereignty Africans began to see missionaries as enemies, which would partly account for Gottlob's lack of support among those he tried to convert (Elphick 1988: 294). Christianity, however, as the advance guard of further economic colonization, was double-edged.

Sexual desire is not allowed any direct expression in the narrative, except in Lyndall's honest desire for the man who impregnates her, but whom she is incapable of accepting because marriage is seen to be part of a network of exploitative economic interests. Desire, however, can work against economic interest, as it does with Gregory Rose, the English settler farmer who abandons his conventional pursuit of Em and cross-dresses to become a nurse when Lyndall is ill and dying. These new forms of fantasy are linked with freedom, the breakdown of the social stereotypes that had upheld the Victorian order in Europe and its colonies, but are shown to have a self-destructive component in their radical subversions. Nevertheless, the transvestism of Gregory Rose is an imaginative nexus that shows how collusive gender constructs are with cultural imperialism, social and economic power. Transvestism has been seen as a defining trope for modernism (Gilbert 1980).

The victimization of Lyndall, however, at the core of the text with its visionary insight into suffering and time, does not subvert a colonial order because the racially othered women in the text, whether "Hottentot" or "Kaffir" women, remain abjected selves and the sycophants and messengers of the farming class. The sign of the South African woman is thus split into a white South African victimized woman and her abject racial Other, the slave. This corresponds to the unconscious projection of a white South African woman writer at the time, torn between her liberal sentiments and her sense of her own lack of education and opportunity for meaningful work and marriage within the colonial order. Desire is sublimated into narratives such as the Hunter Allegory, in which personal suffering is historicized to become that of a pathfinder, a woman who reinvents herself as a historical subject, and rebel leader, within a broader human evolution. *African Farm* records the emergence of historical consciousness in terms of gender and cultural awareness.

The portrayal of the spheres of labour for men and women also reveals the workings of a patriarchal racist society. Waldo is driven to clerical work or work as a brutalized transport rider; Lyndall is refined into meaningless ladylike pursuits; Em is restricted to the nurturing maternal functions of women; Gregory Rose has to disguise himself as a nurse because nurturing was denied to men while being one of the few professional occupations open to women. The African herdsman and his wife have to steal sheep to make a living and are vulnerable to expulsion from the farm; the house servants are foot-washers and mealie-grinders who have to know where their interests lie. The novel shows a time when many certainties are being shaken, however, not just Tant Sannie's conservatism in the face of the railway and new farming methods, but the conventional wisdom that upheld marriage and allied land interests (see Giliomee).[3] As Susan Gubar has pointed out, marriage as miscarriage, and the figure of a dead baby are used in the Victorian Künstlerroman "to articulate the competition between artistic production and biological reproduction" (30).

In the South African version, new European presences are undermining the old order with a more shameless exploitation; the Khoi woman's role as interpreter and translator between Tant Sannie and Blenkins heralds a time when such a position between Boer and British might prove to have some leverage and power. A South African racial conglomerate, with imperfect language ability and skills in communication, and with a small centralized élite based on ignorance, censorship, religious fundamentalism, racial exclusion and cooptation is illustrated on a South African farm in the 1860s, the microcosm of the state that would be further consolidated in 1910, at the formation of Union. Even the missionary class, as in Schreiner's own family, could be seduced to the Diamond Fields to find the promising new wealth of mineral discovery that Otto dreams of on the night he dies: "He comes back one day with gold and diamonds" (85).

Much has been made of the way in which Schreiner challenges the boundaries of conventional narrative in *African Farm*, her mingling of genres such as farce, broad comedy, dreams, didactic allegories, and social realism (Blau DuPLessis, Clayton, Gorak, Monsman). The first section of the narrative uses religious typology and ritual to enact Waldo's crisis of faith and Blenkins's appropriation of religious ritual and texts for his own opportunistic ends. Part 2 of the novel shows how a continual concern with storytelling itself runs parallel to an aborted entry into adult life and underlines the healing functions of narration. Gregory and Waldo return to the farm to tell stories or write letters, thus showing how oral and literate modes commingle in African culture.

While Schreiner uses her preface to the second edition to rebut the errors and false expectations of an English readership, she obviously feels that she has to honour the commitment of a South African novelist to the actual "grey pigments" of the social landscapes around her. Yet this realism has to be used to display the arbitrariness of life and its disarray, "the method of the life we all lead", and the lack of proportion and absolute justice. All of the genres she utilizes function as part of this functional realism, a realism that honours the contradictory, violent, tragi-comic impulses of South African colonial life at a particular moment, when new aspirations were coming into conflict with an established agrarian order and its self-protective norms. The conspicuously non-realistic allegories , "Times and Seasons" and "The Hunter" allegory, cast their light over the whole narrative, underlining the phases of individual life as allegories of a new national consciousness then coming into being around an industrial order. In this emergent consciousness new forms of gender awareness and racial opposition are being forced into being in the mills of industrial competition and capital development. Allegory, as Michael Chapman has recently argued, is one of the narrative genres that has a wide currency in Southern African fiction, especially if it has a politically purposive function. The Hunter allegory, with its emphasis on long suffering, human connectedness in struggle and minimal, difficult historical gains can now be read as an allegory of South Africa's long struggle toward democracy and the sacrifice needed to achieve it.

The Story of an African Farm adapts the European genre of the socially realistic Bildungsroman to the requirements of a visionary imagination working organically within the tensions of a South African society based on inequality, slave ownership, and multiple inequalities of power. The two sections of the novel allow Schreiner to contrast farce and tragedy. The allegorical interpolations, traces of a mythic oral tradition, question the relevance of social realism and the European Bildungsroman to a South African environment and valorize the power of dreaming. The "formal consensus" of the linear realistic novel, which marked a European social consensus, is ruptured by this foundational colonial text (Ermroth). The didacticism of the allegories and of the text generally, which Schreiner saw as evidence of her own intellectual isolation, relate the novel to the "dissertation novels" of first wave feminism (Broe 9).

The representation of indigenous communities reveals competition and forms of alliance; the double male/female protagonist structure allows Schreiner and her reader to dream through imagined male and female selves in the Cape colony at mid-nineteenth century. There is no integration of the main protagonists into colonial society; the patterning of the novel is toward disappointment and death, not social integration. Adults are not the custodians of cultural values but tyrannical representations of an authoritarian society or unable to assert their faith in practical forms of assistance. Nevertheless the impersonality and assurance of the overall narrative tone has an integrative force; the two sections of the narrative and its divergent internal genres are both discontinuous and part of a broader African dream, like Waldo's daydream lying on the red sand of the Karoo. Utopian pressures have fuelled social change in South Africa over the generations.

The Story of an African Farm exhibits some of the features of cultural hybridity and transfer in that it draws on a Western archive in its epigraph and intertextual references to the Bible, John Stuart Mill and liberal enlightenment, but also invokes African ritual in Waldo's sacrifice in the Karoo, and in his rough memorial carving for his father's grave, a token of ancestor worship. The deaths of Waldo and Lyndall could be seen as a broader narrative reworking of sacrificial rituals, the deaths required to regenerate the land at the end of the novel. This ritual pattern would later be reworked in Nadine Gordimer's *Burger's Daughter*. "Land", such a crucial site of conflict and signifier in colonial history generally, but more specifically the special site of racial dispossession in South Africa, thus has a wider significance than the farm, as Waldo realizes when returning from a journey, as the "brown plain" he has been riding over becomes recognizably first "the home farm" and then "the homestead". Different degrees of cultivation and social order are revealed here, with the homestead as part of a man-made social order that can change, while the "brown plain" connotes both the African earth, the people who have always lived upon it, and a principle of faith that Waldo invokes in his sacrifices and carvings, broader than the Calvinist teachings of guilt, predestination and punishment.

It is this broader "land", with its indigenous plants and trees, that effloresces at the culmination of the narrative, when the drought breaks. *African Farm* thus reveals certain limitations on the English colonial imagination that portrayed talented white first generation South Africans as the victims of the social order, while orchestrating at the level of landscape and metaphor the broader community and land that might eventually be returned to its people, but that certainly belonged to them spiritually. Schreiner's transfer of indigenous artistic power, Romantic imagination and spiritual strength to a male protagonist, Waldo, images another gender transfer, of her own female identity to a male figure, reversing at the level of narrative the gender switching of Gregory Rose within the text. These processes suggest that in a new, creative order men and women need to imagine and inhabit each other's gender roles and their constraints in order to dismantle some of the restrictive force of the social construction of sexuality.

Schreiner's other significant but incomplete novel, *From Man to Man* (posthumously published in 1926), does not offer an allegory of national identity at the moment of transition from a rural to an urban order. Instead it uses two sisters as protagonists within English colonial life, showing a transition to forms of metropolitan society, one in middle-class Cape Town, the other in a seedy London boarding-house milieu in which "Baby-Bertie", the younger sister, becomes the sexual possession of a wealthy Jewish diamond merchant. The two Sisters, Rebekah and Bertie, perfectly internalize and act out what Teresa Brennan has called the foundational fantasy of the modern capitalist order, the splitting of female identity into an idealized and degraded aspect. Bertie is seduced by an English tutor who represents, as he does in *African Farm* and in Pauline Smith's *The Beadle* (1926), an exploitative sexuality divorced from conscience. This exploitative sexuality in turn symbolizes the depredations of British capitalist interests in South Africa and the tussle over mineral wealth which led up to the Anglo-Boer War of 1899-1902.

Nevertheless, Schreiner's unfinished novel had its ideological roots in first wave feminism, which argued that the married woman and the prostitute represented two faces of the same coin, an argument that Schreiner extended and substantiated in her nonfictional work, *Woman and Labour* (1911). Only labour and training for labour would give women economic equality and the equality within marriage that could remove a debilitating dependence. Extended within the social world that she creates in *From Man to Man*, these feminist insights are linked to historical allegory, as it is only when an English South African woman, Rebekah, becomes the owner of her own small farm that she is made into an economic agent independent of her unhappy marriage. The farm that she runs does not depend on slave labour, and she develops an insight into the exploitative uses of "Coloured" labour ("Coloureds" being the mixed descendants of whites, Khoikhoi/Hottentot and slaves) in the Cape Colony. These insights are tied to her growing awareness of the ways in which the double moral standards of sexual behaviour for men and women disadvantage married and single women alike, breaking the allegiances between women that could foster forms of collaboration, and creating further barriers to an understanding of gender structures. Rebekah creates an adoptive family of racially diverse children who have to develop tolerance and an understanding of racial bias, even though the mother of her adopted child, who has had a sexual relationship with her husband, is portrayed as racially inferior. The liberal model for race relations still holds in *From Man to Man*, but the main abjection portrayed by the two sisters is one of gender, not race, and as such it has a wider reach than South African national realities, portraying the debilitating polarity within female identity that constitutes the defining condition of patriarchal capitalist modernity and its unconscious.

The story of Bertie, however, also serves as an allegory of the developing relationship between foreign capital and indigenous resources within South Africa. The figure of a stereotypical Jew is used to image both the mercantilist ethic that developed around the Diamond Fields and the European interests that took South African wealth back to Europe. Bertie, once she loses her virginity to her visiting English tutor, becomes worthless goods on the marriage market, and in London she sinks into a depressed torpor caused both by an exile from a landscape she knows and loves, and an exile from respectability in marriage. The norms of respectability in South African smalltown society cut deeply into her life, as her role as seamstress and domestic help to her relatives ends when they hear the gossip that pursues her. In *From Man to Man* religious norms are not central as an issue of spiritual life, but in the form of social norms and hypocrisy, and in the very idealism with which men like Bertie's suitor view her: "the one absolutely spotless, Christ-like thing I have known.... the eternal virgin mother!" (122). Rebekah tells Bertie's suitor that her sister has only "the life of the personal relations" open to her, and is like an aloe that bears only one flower. Rebekah clearly corresponds to the many-sided woman who is like a mimosa-tree, from whose "old dead stem sprouts have sprung" even after the main stem has been chopped down (121-122). These images of organic life and South African vegetation form a rich tapestry throughout the text, and are used to suggest forms of persistence and renewal within women's lives. Even the incompleteness of the novel leaves Bertie's life open to further invention and revisioning, a process visible in Schreiner's letters and journals (Beeton, Rive).

Janet Galligani Casey has pointed out that *From Man to Man* is a kind of storehouse and metanarrative, offering insight into the "struggle for new forms of narrative articulation that characterizes the premodern moment" (125). The teleology of realism is overthrown, and the multiple storytelling modes described and enacted within the text show the reflexivity of Schreiner's concern with narrative in relation to the South African social order. Some of the heroic female stories that the child Rebekah enjoys and tells her imaginary baby reinforce the racial phobias of colonial South Africa and imperialism; her later letter to her husband and adult allegories to her children are non-fictional and abstract, concerning issues of gender and racial power. Casey sees this narrative development within Rebekah's modes of storytelling as constituting " a constantly shifting narrative landscape" signifying a freedom from imperialist and patriarchal attitudes (129). *From Man to Man* becomes "the structural equivalent of the novel's thematic resistance to oppressive social and political constraints" (129). The novel displays a tension between private and public modes of writing, and displays the struggle of a woman writer in a liminal position to record her liminality yet have access to the rational discourse that was the dominant code. The white/black dynamic (of the slave narrative) is displaced by a male/female one (132). While Casey sees Schreiner's oscillation between fictional and allegorical genres as related to a dichotomy between self and other, this oscillation could also be read as an attempt to explore within her writing both the gendered dichotomy of mother/prostitute and the racial dichotomy of the Western discursive modes of literacy and African orality. These complex allegiances are worked out more completely in Rebekah's futuristic allegory to her children of a projected new wave of colonization by a technologically superior white race, which stands in relation to white South African colonizers as they did towards the "savage" races of the subcontinent. In this didactic interpolation the adult Rebekah contextualizes her earlier responses to the indigenous peoples, and invokes a broader principle of human continuity and ethical tolerance to endorse acceptance of diversity and common origins.

From Man to Man differs from *The Story of an African Farm* in that it incorporates Schreiner's own experience of exile in England. Not only was she recasting the novel when she was actually living through her own exile and depression in England in 1883 and 1884, but her post Anglo-Boer War years in South Africa and her own marriage and its partial dissolution from 1894 to 1911 gave her opportunities for further revisions. According to her husband, S. C. Cronwright-Schreiner, he had typed her revised "Prelude" and the first six chapters at Hanover in 1901 and 1902. The manuscript that runs to an incomplete Chapter 13 was sent to him by Olive from Woodstock, Cape Town, in 1911, when she was away from their home in De Aar, two years before she separated from him and went to live in England. His account of the manuscript and his attempts to be faithful to her intentions dwell on her failure to complete the book and reveal that there was one later fragment he did not publish (see S. C. Cronwright). This story of the novel's provenance and manuscript history reinscribes the mechanics of marital dissolution within the story of Rebekah and Frank, and her manuscript sent to Cronwright becomes her own long letter to her husband.

Schreiner's own years in London from 1881 to 1889 brought an understanding of emotional ties to a South African landscape and past, of the metropolitan patriarchal norms and social codes that had been exported to the colonies, and an ability to see commonalities that are expressed in the final chapters of *From Man to Man*. Bertie's story thus illustrates a "gendered dissonance in the dominant culture" (Broe 5) and the origins of colonial conditions in Victorian England. Bertie lives in a boarding-house with a fly-spotted portrait of Queen Victoria on the wall, a matriarchal queen who presided over English codes of marriage and chastity. Rebekah's mature insights incorporate a specifically racialized understanding of power imbalances and the need for a new society based on multi-racial tolerance and acceptance. She reaches that understanding only after she has worked through the gender inequalities of her own marriage, and reconstructed it on terms of public morality but sexual nullity. The pact she forces her husband into gives them both freedom but it cancels the sexual union that marriage is meant to represent. She gains intellectual clarity and economic independence, suggesting how difficult it was, and still is, to maintain marriage on terms of equality for men and women.

The final chapters, with a science fiction fantasy, break a barrier into a new mode, much as Doris Lessing's later space fiction would supersede her own working through the violent racial legacy of Southern African colonialism in the *Children of Violence* novel sequence. *From Man to Man* also rehearses some of the fictional thinking about the poetics and politics of race, gender, and exile that Nadine Gordimer would do in *Burger's Daughter* in 1979. For a South African novelist after the Soweto Revolt of 1976 the worldly sexual affair in Europe of the protagonist, Rosa Burger, is rejected for the political affirmation of her return and her own imprisonment. *From Man to Man* works out the terms of the prisons of gender and race differently, by constructing a narrative of two sisters, the younger of whom becomes a virtual prisoner of sexual exploitation in London, and is passed "from man to man" both across the South African border and within England when she is almost seduced by her Jewish keeper's nephew.

Bertie is the colonial sexual surplus that images capitalist modes in sexual terms, and also the prostitute and sensual woman that her older sister, Rebekah, searches for desperately after her disappearance. This search is a symbolic representation of the desire to reconcile female unconscious needs under patriarchy and capitalism. Rebekah's last child is renamed Bertie and thus her abandoned sister (with the name also connoting a shadowy male persona) is symbolically reabsorbed by the narrative and her own , now matrilineal, family structure.

In the last chapter of the novel, "The Verandah", the narrative voice moves freely between male and female personae, as Mr Drummond, the husband of Rebekah's earlier rival for Frank's affections, takes on the role of a writer very like Rebekah and Schreiner herself, encapsulating her own crucial experiences within writing and publishing. He is a male double with Rebekah's hands and mind, and thus sexual identity is symbolically deconstructed and liberated, even though an element of narcissism is evoked in the doubling of Rebekah's identity in Drummond, suggesting a recurrence of the mirror stage of the Lacanian imaginary. This restless movement between fixity and flux characterizes Schreiner's narratives, and is emblematic of her cultural position as a white female English-South African, living and writing on a cultural and racial boundary that marked surplus and lack, privilege and inferiority, Europe and Africa.

Whereas Schreiner was an early interpreter and cultural commentator between England and Southern Africa, Pauline Smith conceived of her writer's role more narrowly and regionally, as the fictional historian of the poor white community of the Little Karoo, an area bounded and culturally isolated by mountain ranges. She further distances her idyllic, symbolic world by using the technique of the "distant mirror", setting her story back in time to a pre-Anglo-Boer War settled rural community marked by the history, faith and cultural habits of the Great Trek.[4] Yet her aims as a writer are shaped by the tensions engendered between Boer and British by the Anglo-Boer War, and she conceived of her fictional project as one of cultural healing of post-war cultural tensions. Her stories and novel would be a source of knowledge and sympathy for the Afrikaner poor whites, and thus a corrective to British cultural supremacy in South Africa. Her conscious aims as a writer were thus in line with the traditional roles of women as healers and compassionate intermediaries. As with Schreiner's texts, the competing claims and modes of existence are those of the main European settler communities, the English and the Cape Dutch, with the indigenous people as shadowy servants incorporated into Christian servanthood. Smith's gentle ironies indicate that the best these servants could pray for was to be better servants. At the end of the novel, though, it is a white woman and an African servant, Ophelia, who deliver Andrina's child together. The Shakespearean reference, and the inter-racial collaboration that the birth and midwifery represent, binds the healing of the Oedipal situation that rests on her natural father's rape of her mother, Klaartje, her own rejection by Henry Nind, and her jealousy of his English wife. Lacan suggests that the resolution of the Oedipal situation marks the passage from nature to culture.[5] Thus the ending of The Beadle announces a transition from a violent passional world (the world of uncontrolled sexuality) to a cultural and social order which excludes the English as imperialists. This is in keeping with the movement of Afrikaner nationalism and cultural assertion at the time.[6]

Smith's stories in *The Little Karoo* and her 1926 novel, *The Beadle*, are allegories of an emergent early twentieth century Afrikaner community struggling towards literacy and education, and recovering from the effects of a war based on economic interest in the newly discovered mineral wealth of Southern Africa. She mines the spiritual torments of a people enmeshed in an unforgiving Puritan ethic, and reveals how that ethic can be transformed by the Christian compassion and endurance which also lurk within it. The settled rural order she knew is presented as civilized and courteous, but the slave order and the slave bell mimic the historical processes which generated the Great Trek. The slave bell now serves as the bell which summons Christians to church at "Harmonie", the Cape Dutch farm that symbolizes a pastoral order (see Driver, 1983, Introduction). The sexual/romantic transaction which makes up the plot of *The Beadle*, the seduction of a young Afrikaner girl, Andrina, by an English pupil farmer, Henry Nind, is embedded in the narrative of her mother Klaartje's generation. This story is skilfully revealed in a pattern of suspense and confession alternating with Andrina's own movement toward sacraments of sexuality, love, religious faith, abandonment and childbirth.

In Smith's novel, unlike Schreiner's, there is a community that offers forms of mediation and healing: the story of Andrina's mother, her rape by the beadle, flight to a nearby town, illegitimate childbirth and death, is partly healed by the story within the story, of Andrina's spiritual survival, the birth of her child, and her reconciliation with her natural father, now confessed and revealed, the beadle, Aalst Vlokman. At the end of the novel three generations of single people form a new family, mainly because Andrina's lucid faith and strength have never separated bodily from spiritual love. The redemption of the older generation by the younger allows the "love story" to allegorize the damage and the potential healing of Afrikaners, and South Africa, after a damaging war. *The Beadle* thus affiliates itself with an emergent Afrikaans poetic and aesthetic at the time.[7] Its movement across a linguistic boundary, in the errors and translations of the characters and the narrative idiom which mimicked and transgressed the speech habits of both linguistic communities, enacts a new cultural synthesis, that of a bilingual white nation. As Benedict Anderson points out in *Imagined Communities*, "Afrikaner nationalism was pioneered in the latter nineteenth century by Boer pastors and litterateurs who in the 1870s were making the local Dutch patois into a literary language and naming it something no longer European" (75). While Schreiner uses Cape Dutch satirically, Smith's narrative cements Anglo-Afrikaner alliances after the Anglo-Boer War and thus "its capacity for generating imagined communities" builds "particular solidarities" (133). These solidarities undergirded the racially exclusive state that had been forged at the Union of two provinces and the two former republics in 1910. Andrina's Anglo-Afrikaner child symbolizes the white South African nation that was separating itself from British imperial power and would take up into itself the Afrikaner rural underclass once it migrated to the city.

The tropes of *The Beadle*, illegitimate sexuality and childbirth, work affirmatively in terms of gender, though the broken families of both generations indicate the social realities of a poor white community, and the depredations and family costs of war. Andrina discovers her own adult beauty in a forbidden mirror, image of the sexual repression of the Afrikaner Calvinist faith and of her passage into the socially symbolic order. Her lover is a careless Englishman who returns to his own culture and people, so her sexual transaction is fragmented and incomplete. Moreover, her unconfessed father, the beadle, breaks a mirror at the end of Part Two, suggesting his own split identity between church disciplinarian and secret rapist, an unconfessed father who seeks to act as marriage broker. These multiple split identities function as the unconscious of the slave-owning colonial order, a punitive religious code and the aftermath of war between Europe and South Africa. They suggest the deformation of white colonial consciousness much discussed by analysts of colonialism (Mannoni, Memmi). The final scenes of the novel are redemptive and evoke partial healing into family and Afrikaner nation across three generations. Andrina invites the "Ou-Pa" in to see his grandchild, and thus enters the social order in a displaced patriarchal scene in which she encounters her own father for the first time as he encounters his grandchild. This scene symbolizes the cultural healing of Afrikaner generations after the European invasion of war, as well as the psychic integration of sexually split and repressed identities, the unconscious of an emergent white South African nation.

The courage and endurance of Andrina are the catalysts of healing, and thus Smith shows a woman survivor rather than a casualty, able to "bear the unbearable", which is what people do during wartime, and times of private abandonment. Andrina's story is also the invented emotional life of a "poor white" Little Karoo girl and single parent, anticipating the narrative depth a later writer like Bessie Head would give to the women in rural African villages in Botswana. These "poor whites" who worked as sharecroppers and part-farmers suggest the class divisions within Afrikanerdom, and that the victims of land dispossession were not always African. Novels of strong survivors, especially single mothers, can be read as novels of feminist consciousness despite the apparently conservative thrust of Christian ideology. The Englishman's first sight of Andrina is in the pantry, framed by bars, which represents her as a gentle prisoner of the domestic codes of farm life, within which she functions as a servant and childminder. The farmhouse in these early South African novels is a metaphor of memory, as Homi Bhabha has suggested (12), but in both of these novels women are at times imaged as prisoners within the farmhouse, as prisoners of gender and cultural placement. "The recesses of the domestic space become sites for history's most intricate invasions" (Bhabha 9).

Schreiner and Smith thus create narratives of sexual illegitimacy at different historical moments. *African Farm* could be considered a postcolonial novel contesting imperialism, whereas *The Beadle* works within a South African community as a given, and demonstrates the inner linguistic divisions of South African white nationalism. Schreiner's narratives are rooted in the 1870's and 1880's and typify frontier rawness and struggles between competing interests, while Smith's 1926 novel evokes healing within a pre-Anglo Boer War family to suggest ways in which individual women and competing cultural communities are healed and restored after conflict and loss. Lyndall dies after looking into a mirror and seeing her own isolate self; Andrina lives on with her child and regained father in a partially restored community. Andrina's sacrament dress is made from material bought at the "Jew-woman's" store, a woman representing the displaced refugees of Europe in the Little Karoo. Cycles of displacement and war are thus evoked and Europe is constructed as a zone of both imperialists and refugees. There is no absolute binary between Empire and colony, Europe and Africa. The language lessons described in *The Beadle*, prefigurative of love, reveal how Pauline Smith's text works between interpretive communities while showing the power imbalances that skew the text towards European privilege and Afrikaner female abandonment. Though Andrina is an Afrikaner, she also represents a servant class. Such multiple representations undermine any simple linear allegory of nationalism or imperialism.

Female sacrifice and survival stand over against each other in *The Story of an African Farm* and *The Beadle*, but both enact psychic movements through narrative that imagine stories the nation was telling itself between industrial modernity and the Anglo-Boer War. In both cases, the problematic position of women caught between the private history of love and sexuality and the public world of aggressive economic interests and military struggles is evoked. Schreiner's text does this by way of formal ruptures of the realistic Bildungsroman, Smith's by encapsulating her narrative within a smoothly crafted pastoral idyll whose historical roots in slavery could not be forgotten, because they were the prehistory of the new wave of dispossession that constituted the contemporary moment of the novel's creation. The double plot of *The Beadle*, with a rising movement in Andrina's story running parallel and alternately to the suspense plot of the beadle's crime and confession, is cathartic in that both generations' stories are healed, insofar as they can be healed, in the final scene. Schreiner and Smith's texts reveal the complicated position of women in narratives of nation, functioning as signs of vulnerability, recovery, loss and healing. Female protagonists allegorize the constraints and the freedoms of cultural codes as South African national identities and white hegemony were being created across linguistic boundaries at the turn of the century, in the wake of the wars that laid down the lines of the modern industrial nation.

"Women's narratives", as Bhabha has suggested, offer us "the affective, historic memory of an emergent public sphere" (1994: 5). At the turn of the century the emergent public sphere in South Africa was conceived of as white settler nationalism in which bilingualism played a constructive role. Schreiner and Smith offered narratives of identity in which women played a number of roles with different degrees of power within the farm hierarchy. Their white female protagonists, however, are both abandoned to give birth to their children in difficult, isolated conditions, and their suffering symbolizes the problematic relationship between sexuality and women's social existence even though their stories "structure the nation's biography" (Anderson 205). The construction of women as illegitimate subjects in both novels, whether English or Afrikaans, and irrespective of class, reveals the extent to which the nation was being constructed as a domain of male privilege as well as a racially ordered white-controlled state.

Chapter Four
Plaatje's *Mhudi*: Ambivalent Alliances and African Humanism

> That Creator who created,
> created heaven.
>
> This maker of the stars, and the Pleiades.
>
> A star flashed forth, it was telling us.
>
> – Ntsikana, "Great Hymn", translated from the Xhosa by J. K. Bokwe

Sol Plaatje's *Mhudi* is generally seen as the first South African novel in English by a black South African, and its late publication (1930, after being written in 1917) is in itself a sign of the constraints under which Plaatje laboured.[1] Plaatje subtitled Mhudi "an epic of native life a century ago". Solomon Tshekisho Plaatje (1876 – 1932) was a formidable writer and activist, a political journalist, pamphleteer, translator of Shakespeare into Sechuana, co-creator of the first Sechuana phonetic reader, writer of a Boer War Diary and a moving account of African dispossession under the 1913 Land Act, *Native Life in South Africa*.[2] He was a social worker, a literate representative of the Barolong people, and General Correspondence Secretary of the South African Native National Congress formed in 1912 (later the ANC). He twice went on delegations to London to protest the betrayal of the African people by the formation of a white South African Union in 1910 and the land dispossession of the 1913 Land Act. These protests rested on both the service done by African soldiers in the First World War and the basic rights of Africans to the franchise and their land. *Native Life in South Africa*, based on Plaatje's disheartening tour through the affected areas, records the way in which African people, cattle-owning pastoralists like the Cape Dutch Boers, were turned into nomads, cattle-owners with no land, and also forbidden to buy or hire the land on which they had previously farmed. These mechanisms, together with taxation systems, drove Africans off their land and into the cities where their labour was needed. As Bessie Head, one of Plaatje's literary inheritors, wrote in her preface to a later edition of *Native Life*, Plaatje recorded in it the social and political upheaval of a whole people designed to make them into a "landless proletariat".

Plaatje's novel, *Mhudi*, is the literary equivalent of *Native Life*, ironically but strategically cast in the European genre of a pastoral historical romance, in which Plaatje uses the earlier wars and migrations of the "mfecane" or "difaqane" (a term used for the implosions of tribal conflicts and their effects in central and Southern Africa), and the first contact between the Barolong and the Dutch farmers of the Great Trek in the 1830s, to comment on the vast processes of social displacement and land dispossession which occurred in his own time. [3]The "distant mirror" of the African tribal wars which swept across central Africa, in which the warlike Matabele demanded fealty and taxes from the peace-loving Bechuana, and were in turn ousted by an alliance of Barolong and Trekker forces, is used to refract a continental history of colonialism and to prophesy further displacement (see Cowart). The three main features of nineteenth century history noted by Marks and Atmore are all fictionalized in *Mhudi*: the nature of pre-capitalist formations, how these were affected by colonial penetration, and the impact on Africans of the colonial experience and methods of social control (2).

There are many versions of the African *mfecane*, and it is constantly being reinterpreted by historians. Most of them agree that it "was not a solely Zulu-inspired upheaval" (Hamilton 34), as this account has been used by white settlers as a justificatory myth for unequal land distribution and white settlement. In this version, the land claimed by settlers could be seen as waste, unoccupied land (Hamilton 16). Some apartheid apologists claimed that the *mfecane*, an internally motivated series of wars among tribes, "had created a pattern of settlement which formed the basis for the Bantustans of grand apartheid policy", i.e. the homeland system (31). Recent historians have wanted to highlight the relationship between colonial history, slave raiding, and the *mfecane* (Cobbing in Hamilton 391). Mazisi Kunene argues that "the Zulu state, far from being a destructive force, was a stabilizing factor in the whole Southern African region" (35). In this quest to establish a just balance between African and European agency, it is necessary to see "the complexity of relations of domination, subordination, resistance and interaction within and between the various societies of precolonial South Africa" (Hamilto. 8). Plaatje's narrative exists at the fulcrum of this debate, showing us a complex picture of negotiation, interaction, group and individual responses, commentary and reinterpretation of the distant and immediate past. His account fits the recent deconstruction of the *difaqane* by Margaret Kinsman, that it was in fact "a string of superficially disconnected raids" (364), but also shows relationships between broader colonialism and internal displacements.

Plaatje's use of the past is part of a process of indigenous cultural assertion. As Es'kia Mphahlele has pointed out, all of the black South African writers of the early twentieth century were concerned with a double process in relation to the historical and legendary past: going "back in history in order consciously to come to terms with the African's traditional past that was still alive in his time", and using the literary reconstruction as " a source of inspiration" to contemporary readers (1992: 16). Plaatje is one of the forerunners of modern African creative writing which often "focuses on the historical-legendary past of the societies involved" (Gerard 40). As literacy was bound up with the Christian missionary enterprise, and Christianity the only access to any form of modern learning, "literacy became the exclusive privilege of a few Christian converts and their progeny" (Jordan 37). This process of acculturation, which created certain schisms in African communities, with the educated class sometimes becoming the "ears of the government" (Jordan 78) and being mistrusted as a result, also produced the first exemplars of a syncretic African fiction which would expose and contest colonialism and racism. Albert Gerard has called syncretism "the linguistic aspect of acculturation" and suggests that it be seen as part of the global progress of literacy, education and the gradual democratization of culture (1980: 24). It generates "a new, forward-looking form of cultural nationalism" (24).

"Traditional African literature," as Mazisi Kunene points out, is rooted in the everyday and "is about concrete events, concrete situations, and is therefore firmly rooted in historically traceable events" (Kunene 27). Plaatje draws on a historical incident, the 1830 murder of two of Mzilikazi's tax collectors, as the genesis of his plot. This incident highlights both the internal system of fealty and tax of precolonial African society, and allegorizes the contemporaneous grievances against the colonial taxes levied to ensure migration and a labour supply" At the same time it is made clear that such incidents were common, that oral memory is unreliable, that stories are changed in their transmission across time, ethnic and cultural difference, and linguistic boundaries (Mphe). The narrator is presented as someone who has listened to the conflicting tales of others; as a persona, "the Writer" (Plaatje 81), a literate, Christianized scribe of an oral tradition. Plaatje 's attempts to capture "varieties of contributions by different authors" are based on the living debates of an oral Culture (Kunene 25). They are also based on the typical "exchanges of poetic or cultural material" that characterize a pre-literate culture (26).

Plaatje had been a postal messenger, a court interpreter and magistrate's clerk, and at one time an interpreter for British Colonial Secretary Joseph Chamberlain. His position on these boundaries as an interpreter across cultures and languages made his position representative of a Christianized elite, though his formal schooling was limited. He was uniquely positioned to understand the difficulties of translation, the distortions of apocryphal stories, and the ways in which "wild stories" would circulate when "Gossipers wagged their tongues and twisted the story about" (64). These wild stories are told when Ra-Thaga, the hero, and his beautiful Mhudi briefly join a Qoranna clan, whose language of clicks is incomprehensible and at first contemptible to Mhudi. Tribal purity and dignity are praised in the text in a comic description of animal cross-breeding, intended partly to snipe at the colonial appropriation of African women. Yet Plaatje's text makes us aware both of the narrative construction of the history of conflict, the cultural chauvinism that operated between tribes and clans, and the limits of translation. He stresses that different versions of the Matabele/Boer encounter exist (95). He often delays in his narrative and offers conflicting oral versions of incidents whose outcome is later described more fully; yet these different versions form part of the structure of literary fiction. Noble kingly speeches are followed by dissenting voices and interpretations of military raids; others by a confession of the murkiness of the medium, as Chief Moroka's great oratory is followed by the disclaimer that "much of the charm is lost in translation" (97). The text is always acknowledging its position on a cultural boundary between Western and African genres, literacy and orality, communication and misunderstanding.

Mhuidi is fairly well characterized in Odun Balogun's description of Ngugi's fiction as "multi-genre", and indicates in its eclecticism and syncretic mode the later development of the African novel. Plaatje draws on Shakespeare's *Winters Tale* for his dramatic plot about Mzilikazi and Queen Umnandi. The latter is falsely accused of infidelity by her jealous co-wives and hides for seven years, only to return alive amidst jubilation to comfort him with her firstborn son when he flees with his broken people to establish UBulawayo. The Ummandi plot is interrupted in a melodramatic swoon by a messenger which lasts for several chapters until the narrative thread is resumed. The text often breaks into the patterned dialogue of alternate speakers, which, with the opening *dramatis personae*, and the heavy use of incorporated speeches and songs, suggests a play rather than a novel.

The pastoral conventions of Ra-Thaga and Mhudi's "forest home", their idyllic meeting and 'natural marriage outside African custom and ritual, their trials and defeats of dangerous beasts, their journeys across dangerous terrain with many pitfalls, the cross-cultural friendships between Mhudi and the Matabele Queen Umnandi, and the Barolong Ra-thaga and the young Trekker Phil Jay, all work to suggest that piercing historical events have been absorbed by European conventions and language. Mhudi is surpassingly beautiful; plots are laid against Umnandi; the Qoranna chief is a villain who tries to seduce Mhudi. The narrative ends in apparent peace and reconciliation as a young Boer couple bid farewell to their new African friends. Epic conventions are used in the games and preparation for battle, descriptions of battle and heroic exploits, the general elevation of the style and the rebirth of a king with which the story ends.

Within the smooth register of Plaatje's elevated diction and controlled intertwining narratives there is, however, a counter-narrative that bespeaks the realities of African life both in the temporal moment of the action and in the actual time of composition. The novel could be said to set a number of themes going that later became the stuff of African fiction: tribal difference and marital conflict, stock theft and the importance of cattle, the role of prophecy and spirit mediums both in relation to internal battles and colonial contact, the absolute power of African kings and chiefs, the problems of polygamy, jealousy and childlessness for African women, the role of witchdoctors at times of crisis, the animistic world of ancestor worship and the extended family within which people defined their lives. Both Ra-Thaga and Mhudi are orphaned by the Matabele raids against the Barolong, an orphanhood which has a different symbolic register from the white female orphans of Schreiner and Smith, symbolizing as it does the dispossession of family and land for the African majority.

The format and dedications of Plaatje's text, his deference to Lovedale Press, White missionaries and patrons, indicate that his critique of colonialism, European culture and Bantu/Boer contact was forced to be oblique. His style and multiple references to European genres and texts indicate his thorough immersion in English literature, Christianity and western thought, yet there are many signs of his historical allegiance to the history of his own people, both the Barolong specifically and the Bantu peoples dispersed by warfare and then dispossessed of franchise and land in 1910 and 1913. His hero and heroine are Barolong, and their courtesy and love for each other make them an epic African couple symbolizing both the losses and the resilience of the African people as a whole. Yet their reactions both to the Matabele onslaught and the Trekker alliance are different, with Ra-Thaga representing admiration and African naiveté, and Mhudi representing African insight and courage. She first notes brutal Boer treatment of their Hottentot servants, warns Ra-Thaga against the Qoranna chief, and in her dreams and prophecies anticipates future dangers. She also saves Ra-Thaga's life on a number of occasions, and sets out intrepidly to join him at the battlefront with the Matabele. Gender stereotypes are reversed in their marriage, and they are also depicted as individuated lovers heralding a new order free of the traditional customs of polygamy and arranged marriages and of a tribal conglomerate.

A pattern of retribution and prophecy, one of the oral elements within the text, is set up and becomes increasingly complex as the novel progresses. This cyclical structure, part of an African religious ethos, is tied to the appearances of Halley's comet in 1835, foreshadowing Matabele defeat, and in 1910, thought by some African sects to foreshadow the defeat of the whites. This belief led to the killing of 171 adherents to an Israelite sect at Bulhoek.[4] By implication, the final speeches of a deposed Mzilikazi, which hint angrily that the whites would not heed Barolong services and would defraud and disempower them, look forward to the next cycle of fate, history and reversal, when Halley's comet would reappear in 1985, very close to the actual overturning of white hegemony. The cyclical pattern of raid and retribution set up in the opening scenes creates a narrative expectation of further wars and political coups, one which must have been needed at the post-1913 conjuncture when Africans were so radically dispossessed of their rights and land. These narrative patterns are thus part of African resistance couched in millenarian terms.

Symbols of friendship and inter-racial harmony are shot through with irony. Though the final scenes of pastoral harmony carry within them a prospect of future inter-racial alliances, as does the friendship of Ra-Thaga and Phil Jay, the narrative structure and action hint at further reversals of white power. Sarel Siljay is given a "cosy estate" (160) for his services in the military defeat of the Matabele, an ironic reference to the non-reward of the Africans who served in the First World War, and their 'reward' with a loss of their land. When the Barolong first encounter the Boers they say there's "plenty of land for all" (73) but point out that the massive supply of guns outruns Boer needs with regard to hunting and food supplies. Ra-Thaga soon discovers that his friendship with Phil Jay does not prevent him from being attacked by young Boers for drinking from their water supply, and from always being served in different vessels for food at the Boer camp. The future social segregation of the races, so-called "petty apartheid," is contained in this episode. Towards the end of the narrative Ra-Thaga says "You white people have a way of writing down conditional promises and treating them as debts" (164). It is made clear that superior technology, the gun supply, is crucial in frightening the Matabele and in assisting the Barolong against them. The whole plot turns on a pattern of alliance in which the Barolong at first act as guides and hosts to the Boers, who are perceived as strange, hairy intruders: "Dutch emigrants from the Cape Colony" (73), their presence an exotic curiosity and their strange names rendered in phonetic spelling. These good-humoured fictional strategies reverse the home/exotic binary of the imperialist view of the colonial contact period.

The chief allegorization of the post-1913 historical period and its devastating political reversals lies in the massive exodus of the Matabele themselves, a proud people, once conquerors of central South Africa. Their exodus is described when they pack their belongings and prepare to depart northward. Despite their depiction as naked warriors who murder women and children, inspiring terror in the Bechuana, they have been conquered by white gun-power, and the description of their exodus from their terrain invites comparison with the dispossessed African refugees Plaatje encountered in his Southern African travels after the passing of the Land Act. In this way the opening presentation of two refugees from a phase of the *mifecane* wars is taken up in the narrative of the Barolong people, and then in a broader context of African society in southern Africa, prophetically doomed to suffer under the heel of Boer authority. The historical narrative is also tied to the cosmic speculations of Mhudi, illustrating Kunene's thesis that traditional African literature, the oral storehouse on which Plaatje draws, is "a serious system of ethics which it enforces, a preserve of historical events, a body of philosophical speculation, a nexus that produces a logic, not only between past and present generations, but also in the whole cosmic phenomenon" (Kunene 28).

Plaatje is sensitive to the intertwining of gender, racial and cultural issues, and his ironic reversals apply to Ra-Thaga and Mhudi's marriage and gender roles. Just after Ra-Thaga has been advising the young Boer on matters of courtship (in itself a cultural reversal of white norms), Mhudi arrives at the battlefront, and Ra-thaga is angered that his wife has assumed she has a role to play in warfare. Domestic claims intrude on the military life of raids and defeats in this incident and question the value of traditionally separate spheres for men and women. Mhudi is given intelligence, discretion and beauty and, like Plaatje, she often seems to accord with customary deference to hierarchies of power while maintaining her own critical viewpoint. She functions as an analogue for the author working through a Christian mission press and institution. Mhudi and Umnandi discuss together the limitations of the male military ethos. The male world of public power is fractured by dissident voices, humorous tales of cowardice, and the unmanning of the Matabele king by the loss of his favourite wife. Men like Ra-Thaga are shown to enjoy domesticity, privacy and a world of private affection far from the haunts of customary law. As a fable of successful individual, romantic love, *Mhudi* looks forward to Bessie Head's opening story in *The Collector of Treasures*, "The Deep River" (1977) and to her novel *Maru* (1972) both of which use love stories to critique tribal hierarchies. The oral tradition of animal fables is used to illustrate the necessity for co-operation in marriage when Ra-Thaga twists a lion by the tail and Mhudi stabs the animal.

Plaatje's elevated style and the epic, humorous life he gives to this Barolong couple narrate a potential history of resilience and resistance and thus confer agency on people sometimes recorded as helpless victims. The European register of his novel and its complex intertextuality with Western genres are the vehicle of Plaatje 's protest at the massive dispossession of his people after Union and the Land Act, and give it life and voice. It is only when, in retrospect, the love affair of Ra-Thaga and Mhudi is historically framed by the total theft of their land and their rights to the land, that they take on their full meaning as representative actors in a drama wider than their own lives. Mhudi is given some cattle and an old trekker wagon as her reward after the defeat of the Matabele. This transmission of a trekker symbol functions as a final irony in the text: the Barolong woman, who has functioned as an icon of proud national memory and resistance, is now free to become a trekker in the wake of the Land Act. This gift echoes with the ambiguities of gender and racial memory in South African history, but also draws the contours of the African woman's ambiguity, mother and oral transmitter of the nation, but ensconced in a Boer wagon so that she can travel from the land they would later disinherit her from.

Mhudi, as part of Plaatje's socially committed repertoire, was intended to illustrate African consciousness, to "interpret one phase of the back of the native mind", to counter white historiographic bias, and to consolidate Sechuana culture by offering a storehouse of proverbs, oral tales, heroic exploits and the history of his people. His novel exists within a context of cultural advancement, education and prophecy, the roles expected of an African writer, which were broader and more socially defined than those of Schreiner and Smith, and white South African writers generally. His travels in England, America and Canada had shown him the achievements of emancipatory social movements, and the spirit of the early South African Native National Congress was still pacifist, collaborative, and concerned with social upliftment. The tone of this phase is caught in Selope Thema's speech on "how we, as Africans, can live together peacefully with the white population of the land of our birth" (Couzens 1976: 74).

Plaatje demonstrated how the novel could be the oblique vehicle of social protest, even while constrained by the earlier forms of "ethical" censorship, not yet legalized in the Censorship Act of 1931.[5] He also showed how European genres could be effectively mobilized for the purposes of consolidating an indigenous body of historical and legendary narratives, elevating Ra-Thaga and Mhudi to the status of the ancestors of later literary protagonists in African fiction. His use of the family unit as the measure of political conflict, social struggle and the human forces which could resist degradation, anticipates the later social worlds of Peter Abrahams, Alex la Guma and other black South African novelists, even though their picture shows the radical impact of urbanization. *Mhudi* has a deceptively smooth texture, but in its fissures lurks the history of South Africa's major cultural and political dispossession. The charm and humour of its love story are far from the turmoil and distress of Schreiner and Smith's single heroines, and outline the communal resources which would help the African majority to endure the historical events which frame Plaatje 's literary endeavours.

Mhudi has an important place in the debates over settler and black nationalism, and dramatizes a crucial historical juncture both in its inner temporal dimension and its contemporaneous moment. It gave engaging fictional form to the "deep, slow and multi-directional social transformation which over the course of the nineteenth century would break existing social formations apart. The new emergent social groups – the peasant producers, the sharecroppers, the migrant workers – would tie African communities to the European-dominated capitalist structures surrounding them" (Kinsman 393).

Mhudi is also crucial as a literary precursor. Scholar Albert Gerard suggests that "Solomon T. Plaatje and the Dhlomo brothers spear-headed a new trend in the multifarious landscape of South African literature: the outburst of black writing in English after World War II" (Gerard: 1990 113). Es 'kia Mphahlele argues that this early group of novelists and poets, despite their use of lofty Romantic literary vehicles "paved the way to realism in African writing on the sub continent" (1992: 51), a realism which would culminate in with the publication of Peter Abrahams's *Dark Testament* in 1940, shortly after his arrival in England. Abrahams's novels would in turn inspire the next decade – the *Drum* decade – of fiction (Mphahlele 51, Nixon). These linkages are important especially when, as Mphahlele points out, the tradition of writing in indigenous languages, which started out so vigorously, degenerated under Bantu Education into functional writing mainly for school children.

Plaatje's treatment of gender and racial issues is subsumed within an African humanism, but he uses the syncretic traditions of English convention and orality in Africa to point towards the discrepancies between the civilizing colonial project, the motives of the Great Trek's slave-owners, and the displacement of internal African clashes by a more threatening structural Afrikaner dispossession. Ndebele points out that Plaatje ' s "awareness of dialectic in language shows... a potential ability to recognize a similar dialectic in the material transformation of history" (Ndebele (1994: 79) Like Achebe, he uses irony and a pointed deployment of language and convention to show the destructive impact of colonialism on African pre-history, while revealing in his depiction of love and marriage, and a strong collective context, the human resources that would resist that impact. Moreover, in creating an oral narrativet within European conventions, he demonstrated how much could be conveyed of both political critique and an oracular, utopian vision represented by a prophetic female voice. This utopian vision would be considerably darkened in the next two decades under the impact of urbanization and apartheid rule, but its cyclical, long view would eventually prove justified.

Mhudi can also be read as a counter-colonial narrative within the debates on narrative, history and South African literature that cluster around the difaqane. Norman Etherington points out that there are three templates governing narrative structure in standard accounts of the difaqane and the Great Trek: the onward march of civilization, the growth of a nation and the advance of the capitalist means of production (36). Cobbing suggests that the analytical focus should shift from the aggressive movement sparked off by the Zulu to a period of turbulence resulting from an intensification of intrusive forces stemming from the "advance agents of the world economy" (Etherington 49). The corollary for the Great Trek is that the Trekkers were part of the intrusive process, not weird anachronisms in flight from it (49).

Though Plaatje exploits intercultural humour in his Barolong accounts of the Trekkers, he shows probable historical motivations and alliances between groups. Also, by drawing our attention to the examples of racist behaviour among the Trekkers, in contrast to the love and warfare that dominate the earlier sections of the narrative as romance motifs, he shows how "a fully fledged ideology of race, nurtured in the material conditions of late nineteenth century imperialism, came to be enunciated in South Africa as the ideological means for the reproduction of a particular mode of production" (Wolpe 429).

Threading the story of Mhudi and Ra-Thaga through the difaqane and the contact with the Trekkers enables Plaatje to read back from the post-Land Act period into the story of the eighteen-thirties the consequences of racial attitudes in the formation of Union and the exclusion of African from any franchise, and from their land. The difaqane is then no longer an alibi, a "crafted myth" used by historians to cover up colonial violence (Cobbing 364), but part of an interconnected sequence of contacts and clashes, each with prevailing sets of interests and motives.

In *Mhudi* we see the "beginnings of slow, complex and profound social processes of social and economic transformation in African communities on the highveld. These changes would play an increasing role in shaping African interaction with European merchants and settlers." (Hamilton 365). In its self-reflexive pointers to the construction of narrative by multiple tellers, Plaatje draws the reader's attention to the partisan narratives of history while leaving us in no doubt that those who own the guns generally live to tell the story, and often own most of the land.

Chapter Five
Desire and Transgression: Nationalism, Degeneracy and the 'Miscegenation Novel'

> "A Jew, a half-caste, and a Negro are meeting tonight in a village in Africa." – Peter Abrahams, *Path of Thunder*

South Africa has become notorious for its legalization of racial segregation and its legal bans on sexual relationships and marriages between people of different races. Such formalizations of racial prejudice and cultural taboos were enacted in the Immorality Act of 1927, and later in the Mixed Marriages Act of 1949 and the Population Registration Act of 1950. The legal bans turned on the rigid classification of people into racially demarcated and defined groups and were enacted and enforced more strictly after 1948 when the Afrikaner Nationalist Party came into power. But one of the earliest Afrikaner formulations of inequality occurred in the 1858 Transvaal Republican constitution, when it was ruled that there would be "no equality between coloured (here meaning all 'non-whites') and white inhabitants, either in Church or in State." This Republican spirit in the Afrikaans community turned on a denial of independence and equality for black and coloured South Africans, and was upheld by the Dutch Reformed Church, the theological wing and a segregationist state. Some earlier historians have viewed the Afrikaners as fighters who opened "the anti-colonialist century with their freedom struggle against British colonialism" and who set the example for other colonial peoples (Munger 4). In this view anti-colonialism becomes the seed of Afrikaner nationalism and "the first African country actually to free itself of colonial rule was South Africa" (Munger 4). With the development of African resistance, and the association between the African National Congress and the South African Communist Party, a theory of the South African revolution was developed, mainly articulated by Joe Slovo.

In 1976, when 87% of the land and wealth was white owned and controlled, with puppet forms of "self-government" being promoted in 13 % of the land, Slovo argued that the "white settler oligarchy" (135) that controlled the racial monopoly over all the essential means of production had assumed the functions of the British ruling class. He described race discrimination as "the *modus operandi* of South African capitalism" (118), with legal and institutional domination turning on economic exploitation. The internal settler state was marked by the earlier competition between rival imperialist powers (England and Holland). Within the ideological framework of the South African revolution, the ANC developed a common consciousness "in the face of earlier tribal sectarianism which made foreign piecemeal conquest so much easier" (116), and the SACP promoted the "aspirations of the working class" and aimed to establish a socialist South Africa (116).

These forms of alliance can be seen in the representative alliances described between characters in the work of Peter Abrahams and Alex la Guma, among others. Class and race were seen as the crucial complementary determinants of two streams of revolutionary consciousness, often in alliance, but also in dispute. Slovo suggests that the "theory of internal colonialism" is mainly a useful analogy and shorthand, "to depict the reality of the historically specific race factor" (135). In South African criticism, different weightings and interpretations are given to the factors of race and class, with gender appearing rather late on the critical agenda. Postcolonial critiques have begun to highlight the need for a closer analysis of the forms of colonialism, and their interlocking with forms of state control after independence from imperial powers.[1] In the South African case, there is a high degree of conformity and parallelism between imperial control of the earlier colony and later white settler control of the black majority as a labour resource and a disenfranchised majority.

South Africa can be seen as a zone of "two powerful and competing nationalisms", Afrikaner and African nationalism (Munger 1). Afrikaner nationalism gradually absorbed many English-speakers, the formation of Union in 1910 being carried by a wave of sentiment for English-Afrikaner unity.[2] One historian has described the situation of the English-speaking community as analogous to that of farm squatters supporting the status quo and economic prosperity for a portion of the reward (Denoon 222).[3] In this process of ideological sedimentation, literature played a formative role, with the fiction of Pauline Smith and later Alan Paton helping to weld an English-Afrikaans bilingual cultural identity.

The literature of 'miscegenation' in South Africa is extensive and provides a significant commentary on the practice of mixed-race sex with which the settlement began in the seventeenth century. The existence of the Coloured people is predicated on the history of sex across the "colour line". Sarah Gertrude Millin's 1924 novel, *God's Stepchildren*, is a casebook illustration of the ways in which cultural and racial prejudice could turn on pseudo-biological arguments, and inter-racial sex could be conflated with sexual laxity, promiscuity and degeneration. In this novel, the sins of the Reverend Andrew Flood last across many generations of Coloured offspring who "try for white", fear a "throwback" to "darker blood", and are uneasily caught between black and white aspirations. Adapting the multi-generational novel to racial eugenics and a literary myth that justified segregationist thinking, Millin gave classic form to a white South African habit of mind, which viewed racial dispossession as moral rearmament, and justified political exclusions on the basis of race, for how could degenerate beings aspire to rationality and legal process? Millin's "sins of the fathers" are flooded through future generations; her view is the conservative obverse of Olive Schreiner's liberal epigraph to *African Farm*, that the "whole man is to be found in the cradle of the child".

Millin's narrativization of racial degeneracy as the fruit of sexual sin was the more damaging for being cast in a historical mould, drawing on historical sources and contexts. The sentimentality of the title, "God's Stepchildren", evoking an image of liberal protectiveness and family inclusiveness, is in fact belied by the insistent narrative patterning, generational repetition, and key metaphors of taint and blood-guilt (J. M. Coetzee 1988). *God's Stepchildren* in fact struck a powerful blow for the disenfranchisement of the Coloured people, and its linkage of sexual laxity with interracial sex provides the legitimating framework for apartheid thought and policy. Peter Abrahams sees the novel as stemming a tide of sympathy for the Coloured people after they lost the right to elect one of their group to the Cape Parliament at Union in 1910 and making "'the cult of blood' respectable as a literary commodity" (Abrahams 1953: 58-59; Coetzee 1988: 138). The title also disavows moral responsibility for mixed-race offspring, seeing them as the wards of God but justifying their exclusion from rational social life.

Gareth Cornwell has argued persuasively that the novels of the "tragedy of colour", of which Millin was the chief exponent, represent a domestication of the European novel to local conditions (75). Reacting to the adventure novel and to frontier romance, and attempting to win moral seriousness for a South African national novel tradition, novelists like Millin had "recourse to a typology of character based on ethnicity rather than class" (77). Race becomes the major South African theme and is related to a nationalist cultural project: "through Millin, the white or colonial South African novel tradition articulates its discovery of a national life major enough to measure up to the demands of the imported form of the realist novel" (79). Race is claimed as a major topic in the interests of realism and a self-evident cultural nationalism which is not linked with the racialized basis of the state, but is implicitly seen as ameliorative, as a moral task. Cornwell points out that "The colonial apologist like Millin discovers in the theme of race a moral vindication, a source of social and political identity with the emerging nation-state, a sense of independence from European cultural and intellectual tradition" (79).

Characterization in such fiction is based on biological determinism. 'Destiny' or 'Fate" become actors in these narratives, obscuring the workings of racial typology. Colonial ethnic perspectives on immutable weaknesses and failures attributed to racial heritage are usually vindicated in plot outcomes (81). These inscriptions of a radical racial difference, while disguised as liberal sympathy and the workings of Christian conscience, propped up the white colonial bourgeoisie at a time when masses of blacks and poor whites were streaming into urban centres, and the lines of racial segregationist policy were being laid down. From 1910 to 1948 "the foundations were laid for totalitarian government" and "the white community became infected by a siege mentality" (Denoon 156). These novels reveal the unconscious fears of this "besieged" group."[4] Racial mechanisms become an uneasy substitute for the class distinctions of the European realist novel, and the class and economic anxieties that Millin knew as a child of Lithuanian immigrants at the River Diggings in Kimberley are displaced onto racial hereditary patterns that offer a comforting sense of 'civilized' superiority and certainty. Instead of the European Bildungsroman pattern in which individual moral growth moves toward integration into society through marriage, an original cross-racial sexual liaison or marriage begins a pattern of decline from civilization. The characters have all internalized racial norms as self-defining, and the generational patterning is a powerful ideological tool to justify total social and sexual segregation for the races.

William Plomer's *Turbott Wolfe* (1925) is a liberal attack on white philistine habits of thought in Natal, his home province, on provincialism and racial segregation, couched in a cross-racial love affair, but the novel suffers from the idealization of the ebony maiden, Nhliyizombi, and the protagonist, like Plomer (who would soon depart for England) has his roots in Europe, not Africa. Nevertheless, *Turbott Wolfe* is based on a longing for human connection and spiritual beauty, and it captures the idealistic tone of early opposition to segregationist policy in its "Young Africa" movement and the coinage of "Eurafrica" for the "Coloured" people. Van der Post sees it as a key work in that at last "imagination keeps open house in a divided land" (quoted by Parker, 85-6). Kenneth Parker remarks upon its "style, cosmopolitan panache, and its satiric detachment" and sees it as "a forerunner of the 'liberal novel' and at the same time a critique of liberalism" (86). The critique of liberalism, however, is in part displayed by the prototypical Christian radical, Friston, who advocates miscegenation as an answer to South Africa's political and social problems, and Friston goes berserk, like Van der Post's protagonist at the end of *In a Province*. We are not too far from the forms of dementia associated in imperialist ideology with the costs of "going native".

The Conradian Kurtz paradigm of the representative of civilized ideals who regresses in Africa is another form of the racialized decadence represented in Millin's narratives, and in terms of plot outcomes and narrative trajectory *Turbott Wolfe* props up a conservative politics of race. Racial mixing leads to disaster and Eurafrica cannot take hold in the actualities of relationships. This form of degeneration is based not on a poetics of blood-mixing but on an imperialist ideology which attributes to white consciousness a mental refinement and delicacy which cannot endure the strains of African reality. This is even more evident in Van der Post's *In a Province*, where Coloured sensuality is described in hideously repulsive terms, but it is also clear in *Turbott Wolfe*, where there is a fastidious recoil from female sexuality as such. The political valency of both novels is hard to define because the division of women into noble virgins and whores is racialized, and the revulsion from Coloured women is intertwined with a revulsion against (hetero)sexuality. The modernist cult of aestheticism mingles with a colour-coded South African Puritanism in both novels.

At the same time Plomer, after an early education in England, was in touch with European cultural debates and aesthetics. His first-person narrative within a novel, framed by the confessional structure of Wolfe's narration to someone very like William Plomer in England, is an early experiment in meta-narrative anticipating the self-reflexivity of J. M. Coetzee in the seventies and eighties. *Turbott Wolfe*, and the departure of the young editors of *Voorslag* magazine, Plomer, Laurens Van der Post and Roy Campbell, reveals the limited and frustrated roles of white intellectuals at the time, and the perennial migration of stimulating creative intellects into expatriation and exile, a trend that devitalized South African intellectual life. Though Peter Abrahams also left South Africa for England, in 1939, his departure, after the removal of Cape Coloureds from the Common Voters Roll in 1938, gave him the freedom to create, and to reflect on political and social life in South Africa, and created ties with other forms of racial oppression, so that he calls himself "a Negro", and a child of the "plural societies" in *Return to Goli* (27, 28).

Two novels of miscegenation that narrate the crisis of the post-war period and the Nationalist accession to power are *Path of Thunder* by Peter Abrahams (1946) and Alan Paton's *Too Late the Phalarope* (1953). Both novels move towards a plot climax of destruction, revealing the death drive and anti-humanism of the Immorality Act, but they are very different in their mythologizing of cultural identities and South African racial communities. *Path of Thunder* is the story of an educated Coloured schoolteacher who returns to his Karoo Village of Stilleveld after an absence of seven years, falls in love with the white niece of the Afrikaans farm patriarch, and is destroyed by the love affair. The friendships and alliances of young educated people in Stilleveld symbolize the building of multi-racial alliances, which would gather force after 1948, and the harsh segregationist legislation that would follow. Lannie Swartz is a middle-class literary hero who can quote Pringle, Totius, Steinbeck and Blake, and wishes to serve the rural community of his parents through education. He has been politicized in Cape Town and is a part of an emergent élite. In Stilleveld he forms a discussion group with a young Jew, son of the local shopkeeper, and an African, Mako. They discuss nationalism, the in-between position of the Coloured community, "betweeen two fires" (86), the upward mobility of Coloured people in cross-racial relationships, and their own diverse religious heritages.

These earnest and well dramatized dialogues recall the radical gatherings of George Eliot's *Felix Holt* and look forward to the lively intellectual debates of the South African fifties intelligentsia in Sophiatown, Johannesburg. The intertextual reference to a famous Thomas Pringle poem ("Afar in the Desert"), the "silent bushboy" who accompanies the European settler, shows that Abrahams is aware that he is giving literary voice and intellectual aspiration to a silenced community. Other intertextual references, to Countee Cullen and Blake, build into the novel currents of American anti-slavery and European currents of freedom. Blake's song of innocence is quoted to emphasize the literary representation of a rural Coloured community: "And I plucked a hollow reed/ And I made a rural pen..." (124). Stilleveld is made representative of places where group resistance might soon gather: "A Jew, a half-caste, and a Negro are meeting tonight in a village in Africa" (78). The "cell" of broad-spectrum political resistance is pictured here.

From the outset an air of doom overshadows the budding love affair between Lannie Swartz and Sarie Villier, which is described in romantic terms as a marriage of souls, and a human bond of equality that challenges the racist norms of the white community. Like Smith's *The Beadle*, the plot turns partly on the revelation of an earlier generation's love triangle, in this case a cross-racial one which led to the death of Sarie the first, and the mutilation of the Coloured man involved, now "Mad Sam." Mad Sam is the symbol of the South African unconscious, the fear and violence that underpins racist legislation about human love and sexuality. He acts as a barometer of the new generation's love affair, and the historical trace of South African racial segregation and its violent, mutilating effects. He is loved by Fieta, a strong woman seen as promiscuous by the village. She is torn between the unappealing alternatives of sporadic sexual raids on South African towns, followed by illegitimate children, or her love of a Coloured man who has fallen for a white woman and been punished by white vigilantes. The upward aspirations of Coloured men in both generations serve as a further form of frustration for Coloured women, who can at best be the servants of the white farmers in the "big house on the hill". Nor are they personally helped by people like the English anthropologist with whom Lanny's sister Mabel falls in love, and who carefully explains to her that his love is simply brotherly and humane. The Coloured community is shown as torn in several ways by conflicting gender, class and ethnic conflicts, with the rural Coloureds living in abject poverty. The historical underpinnings of these descriptions are found in Abrahams's account of the location of Albertsville, where his family still lived during his 1953 visit to South Africa (Abrahams 1953: 51).

Path of Thunder is well crafted and told in a lyrical, impressionistic manner against the backdrop of a rural landscape. There are didactic narrative interpolations which set "the valley of the heart" against the literal settlements of Stilleveld and "Mako's Valley", and injunctions to human love against legalized inequality. The Villiers are the first white settlers in the valley, which functions as a microcosm of a South Africa in which legalized racial inequality would soon lead to the Defiance Campaign and more organized multi-racial political resistance. The old aunt, Tante, who holds the secrets of the first generation, and whose memories go back a century to the Trek and the frontier wars, acts as a prophetic voice foretelling the next cycle of retribution, in which the whites would suffer (202). The love affair draws attention to South Africans as one "family", in the sense that for a while Lanny, illegitimate son of the farmer Gert Villier, believes he is thus the half-brother of Sarie, the girl he loves. She turns out not to be a blood relation, but this plot twist underlines the incestuous racial history of the country and the folly of legislating against it. Lanny is an illegitimate child representing the entire 'illegitimate' Coloured community of South Africa and its aspirations, thus his illegitimacy is not a sign of gender protest, like the unwed mothers of Schreiner and Smith, but a sign of a hybrid South African racial history. His love for Sarie is a natural love between equals because they *are* equal, and their love affair is the protest of nature and humanity against laws that seek to undo and deny history as well as humanity. The outcome can only be political struggle, which is articulated by Mako, the African teacher: "There is only the fight to live and be men instead of slaves" (232). Mako's advice to Lanny is to sacrifice personal love for the future, which would be the path that some resistance leaders would later take.

At the end of the novel we are given a newspaper report on the shootout between the lovers and the white overseer of the farm, who is also the informant to the newspaper. The Coloured man is blamed and the white is a wounded hero. This epilogue underlines the cultural and discursive control of the media by a frontier ethos, and by the same whites who make the unequal laws and take the law into their own hands in violent retribution. The newspaper report also makes it clear that Coloured novelists were needed to give the "silent bushboy" a voice and presence on the South African literary stage. The interpretive community is the lawgiving community, and this circular reinforcement of authority shows that history itself is a "saturating hegemonic system" (Said quoted by Hamilton 74).

The climax of Abrahams's novel anticipates the revolutionary policy that Slovo later formulated: "the new society in South Africa will only come through a successful revolutionary assault by the deprived, in which increasing armed confrontation is unavoidable" (113). Abrahams's lyrical humanism has sometimes obscured the inevitable pressure he records in his narratives towards armed and violent confrontation of a racist order (see Soyinka).[5]

Alan Paton's *Too Late the Phalarope* (1953) demonstrates what Hayden White calls the "interest of the dominant social group... in controlling the authoritative myths of a given cultural formation and in assuring the belief that social reality can be lived as story" (White x). By acting as an English-speaking intermediary for the Afrikaner Puritan ethic and its concomitant racism, Paton welds English and Afrikaners into a gruff, sentimental alliance which nevertheless constructed its hegemony on a system of racial exclusions and appropriations. The story concerns Pieter van Vlaanderen, noble scion of a Voortrekker clan, rugby star, police lieutenant, and war hero, who is destroyed by his illegal lust for an African girl, Stephanie, who passes through his authority as a police officer. He is described as "two men", the strong and pure leader, and a darkly brooding man with wilful passions. Thus he represents the sexual repression of a puritanical Afrikaner community. His story and double personality reveal the crack that runs through Afrikanerdom, with its history of public laws against miscegenation but its private pursuit, partly because of the prohibition of desire, but mainly because the structures of power made African women an exploitable resource. Nella, Pieter's wife, is the gentle, respectable mother, and Stephanie the black whore, and thus the doubleness of women replicates the two sides of Pieter's nature and the (im)moral structure of belief on which the capitalist apartheid state rested. However, Stephanie has a child whom she loves and will not give up, but her prison sentences for illegal liquor brewing, often the only source of income for urban African women, are leading to an enforced separation from her child. Africans in the city are shown to become dependent on crime for survival, and to be enmeshed in impossibly contradictory demands. This is the situation that finally destroys the protagonist, because Stephanie uses her knowledge of Pieter's 'crime' to punish the society that will not allow her to keep her child. She is also presented as the initiator of the relationship, as a woman who uses her sexuality for favours from authority.

Paton uses a disfigured spinster aunt as his narrator, a woman hungry for love, whose favourite is her handsome nephew. She represents religious fervour and frustrated desire, and is the female counterpart of the hero Van Vlaanderen, who also craves more passion from his wife and suffers from an ill-defined brooding guilt, even before his cross-racial affair. The context of his adult misery is his frustrated affection for his undemonstrative father, who has punished him as a boy by removing his stamp collection, and with whom he later seeks a reconciliation by presenting him with Roberts's *Birds of South Africa*. The "phalarope" that they never quite see together, and which his father thinks a mistake made by the English author, symbolizes both the elusiveness of father-son love in a patriarchal society and the strained, but potentially harmonious relationships of English and Afrikaans-speaking South Africans after World War II. The construction of masculinity by a Puritan ethos of ruggedness, sporting prowess, military courage and authority is shown to have a cost, in the son's woundedness and his wilful "evil" expressed in his lust for Stephanie.

Because of the spinster narrator the whole narrative is framed as a brooding, self-fulfilling prophecy, and cannot move outside the terms of Afrikaner nationalism and religious conservatism. The hero, Pieter, is cast as the victim of the story and is set up by a junior officer whom he has helped, and an African woman who is afraid to lose her child, and who uses his father's law against him. The clinching evidence of his adultery is a shell brought back to the village by a young girl and given to the servant, Stephanie, and thus the "girlish" side of Pieter, the affective side of his nature which his father sought to repress, takes its revenge. No-one questions the public disgrace and the appropriateness of the punishment, nor the legal terms of the offence. We hear early on of "the great machinery of the law" and "the certitude and majesty of the white man's law" (39), but nothing in the novel is set against the law, nor questions its justice, except the destruction of the van Vlaanderen family.

The historical transactions that created the unequal distribution of land are equally romanticized; there is a "rough track that goes down into the ravine which our forefathers gave to Maduna when he yielded to them" (48). Stephanie is first seen in a wooded ravine under a waterfall, and is associated with a lost childhood, yet the relationship is also seen as defilement, as mere animality, and she is described as " a lost creature" because of her promiscuity. Sexuality is linked with shame and defilement and racial revulsion is naturalized. Pieter, the all South Arican hero and moralist, is linked with " some tragic trouble of the soul" which is never fully explained, and this excess of soul-sickness represents the white South African psyche under segregationist law, though it serves to obfuscate these laws. The subtext seems to be that Pieter is suffering from his father's prohibitions and authority, and that his maleness is fractured in some way: " I wished to God I had been made a woman" (206). Like other Paton heroes, he wounds the women close to him, such as the narrator aunt who dotes on him. There is much inarticulate love between men in the novel, expressing a craving for human affection and closeness, and representing a society which cheats both men and women in its inflexible gender codes and racial exclusions from full humanity.

The form of the narrative is dualistic, with Pieter's grieved and guilt-stricken consciousness presented in italicized narrative sections. The whole novel is an exercise in bilingualism, rendering Afrikaans as English in a stilted archaic syntax, with the original Afrikaans words sometimes being cited, to show the difference and irreducibility of language. Language is thus tied to a national spirit and norms of conduct, to cultural and ethical standards, yet at the same time Paton strives to convey a South African commonality in humour and sport, and in his glossary of terms. *Too Late the Phalarope* carries a burden of feeling that is never quite embodied in the text, but is hinted at, and this burden of feeling seems to relate to family feeling, to affection between Afrikaners and English-speakers, and to the inexpressible love of a father and husband for his children and wife. There is no basis for a critique of the immoral laws that cut into family life and reputation, because of Paton's own exaggerated respect for the law, and his sentimentality about Anglo-Afrikaner relationships, expressed in the South African stamps that are more valuable because "joined together". Only the two main white communities are joined together in this way, however, and their emotions of vulnerability, guilt and remorse are paramount.

Stephanie is the agent of temptation, though her story is informative of the working conditions of African women's lives. She is mainly cast as self-serving and the agent of Pieter's temptation and 'sin'; her consciousness is not rendered. The Afrikaner and African families are presented as mutually exclusive outside the feudal terms of service. Typically, Pieter's reaction to his involvement with Stephanie is to wish her sent away, thus revealing the emotional basis of the separate areas of the later homeland system and the earlier Land Act. The honour and reputation of the white Afrikaner are shown as hollow, for they rest on the sexual exploitation and fragmentation of the African family. Unjust South African laws are read as absolute moral norms by the main characters and the narrator. The awkwardness of the idiom and syntax, however, seem to suggest that the union of English-speaker and Afrikaner, enacted in the author/narrator pact, was a forced one. Paton was seeking creative sympathy with the central Afrikaner myths, and trying to forge a South African national identity which he could not help seeing was built on the unacknowledged humanity and exploitation of women like Stephanie. This sympathy with Stephanie was all the stronger because Paton himself suffered under an authoritarian father.[6]

Too Late the Phalarope relies, like *Cry, the Beloved Country*, on a frustrated tension between judgment and compassion. Paton's novel of interracial sex provides ideological cement for a white power bloc across a language divide, whereas *Path of Thunder* points towards a future of resistance against inhumane laws, and violent revolution. Abrahams foresaw the end of white minority rule in 1953, and predicted that "the end of the century will also see the end of the white minority wielding power, benevolent or otherwise, over the Black majority" (Abrahams 1953: 168).

In retrospect, *Too Late the Phalarope* offers an implicit understanding of the male homosocial bonding which articulated with white South African power, and the way in which the abjected African woman could offer a remedy for the white male wounded by an authoritarian racist order. The mechanisms of social expulsion and shame are presented through the narrator's viewpoint and her links with the Van Vlaanderen family. The novel 's presentation of guilt and expiation is a racialized form of Pauline Smith's depiction of "the beadle", also an icon of community Christianity and respectability who has sinned in private sexual morality against his own Afrikaner tribe.

In Nadine Gordimer's *Occasion for Loving* (1963) the process of resistance is shown to have gone a step further. The activities of the ANC (the "Congress), in which the black South African, Gideon Shibalo, is involved, are depicted as they move towards the imprisonment of resistance leaders after the Sharpeville massacre of 1960, though the main focus is on the white bourgeois order and its shifting morality. There is political debate about the calls for a new All Races convention, labour strikes, and a shift to underground politics. The main focus of the novel is on sexual politics, but the sexual politics of an inter-racial love affair, in Gordimer's hands, are enormously informative of the new ways in which English liberal politics were being tested in the fifties and sixties. Tom Stilwell is an academic engaged in a "history of South Africa from the black point of view" (15) and Boaz Davis is a Jew who has returned to South Africa to research African music and musical instruments. This "black point of view" is equated, in conversation, with "the historical point of view", but the implication is that white academics are uneasily aware of their appropriation of a viewpoint that is not historically their own. The universities are discussing the Nationalist decrees on education, which involve the closing of the universities to 'nonwhite' students.[7] In short , the historical crux of the early sixties is reflected in the growing debate and dialogue about the ethical responsibilities of educated white South Africans, even as these responsibilities are being tested by the passionate inevitability of an inter-racial love affair.

As is customary in Gordimer's fiction, the main narrative trajectory concerns the psychological maturation of a female consciousness, that of Jessie Stilwell, first glimpsed in her mother's garden, a girl who has never been beyond "the flaming angel at the gates" never risked transgression of taboos, who is still held within family resentments and old angers. Jessie Stilwell is in her second marriage, has an awkward relationship with the son of her first marriage, Morgan, and destructive memories of her mother's two marriages. An unsettling incident with her son, who affirms his emergent sexuality by going to a vulgar dance hall, is the first incident to trouble her evasions of her own past. A flashback to her unhappy childhood has her witnessing her mother's "secret shame of unwanted lust" (26). The cross-racial love affair she is about to witness seems to act as the catalyst of memory and forbidden desire which will enable her to move out from under the dead hand of her personal past.

Occasion for Loving applies the novel of European sensibility and shifting consciousness, as developed by Henry James and E. M. Forster, to one of the early crisis periods of modern South African history, the culmination of republican sentiment that led to the establishment of a South African Republic in 1961, and the implications this had for the code of private ethics and detachment from crude "baasskap" (white sovereignty) cultivated by bourgeois English-speakers of liberal sentiment. The Stilwells represent this code, and it is tested by the involvement of their houseguests, Boaz and Ann Davis, in the wife's love affair with a black painter, Gideon Shibalo. Ann Davis has lived in England for years after a Rhodesian childhood, is a child of the moment, beautiful and spontaneous, and apparently without any sense of "the colour bar" which had by then been articulated culturally and legally in South Africa for centuries. She is a later version of Smith's Andrina, who had no "saving sense of sin" and had sex with an Englishman without marriage. Jessie Stilwell, a woman with a dreamy artistic consciousness, is shocked into the life around her by Ann and Gideon's affair, and during a stay at her stepfather's beach cottage the couple come to stay while considering flight from South Africa's oppressive racial laws. In a scene that seems to heal Jessie's wounded fantasy life (the first fantasy, for white South African women, is socially inculcated fear of a black attacker, we are told) she witnesses the impersonality and equality of two bodies after lovemaking:

> She looked with calm a moment at the ancient grouping of the two bodies, the faces flung away from each other, the arms lax where they had been held; all that had been centred rolled apart in sleep. Ann's one brown-tipped breast was pressed out of shape, like her cheek, by the angle at which she lay on her side, with the whole of the lower part of her body swung across as if she were lying face-down. And he lay on his belly with his head over the outstretched arm whose curved fingers, no longer within reach of her head, still conformed to the shape of it. His dark body had a shine going down the curve that followed the groove of the spine to the short, gleaming roundness of the buttocks. Their faces were sweaty. A fly rose and settled indifferently on either (250).

After the beach holiday, the Davis couple retreat into their marriage, and Jessie accepts her son's autonomy, but Gideon Shibalo is destroying himself with alcohol as the novel closes. The white bourgeoisie have closed their ranks, and the class basis of the racial oligarchy is shown to be an overriding determinant. The Stilwells' code of private disagreement with ruling policy, and a European detachment from South African brutality, has come to seem "in danger of humbug" (279). Ann has returned to her husband and carefree globetrotting; Jessie has refreshed and integrated her psychic life in a new way, and Gideon, who has already had a passport refused and an art bursary lost, loses twice over. Jessie has understood the burden of the story:

"so long as the law remained unchanged, nothing could bring integrity to personal relationships" (279). The reader is brought to understand the ways in which apartheid society works when Gideon and Ann drive around the country and are forced into embarrassing and awkward situations through separate amenities, white South African assumptions, and a growing fear of prosecution. Their love affair, for a while played out in an Edenic eucalyptus plantation near a disused gold mine, cannot go on existing merely in privacy, and cannot go public. The development of capitalism is still too firmly wedded to the racialized state that depends on black urban labour for the working gold mines, and the white South African who invades their Edenic picnic spot represents this concatenation of Realpolitik, urbanized white South African power, and finance: " a farmer, in a good gray suit... on his way to the lawyer or the bank..." (232).

Occasion for Loving works along a boundary between Europe and Africa, demonstrating that the novel of sensibility and private consciousness, represented by Jessie Stilwell and her reading (De Chardin, Mann, Conrad) is inevitably changed in South Africa by the pressure of new content. Like Gideon's paintings, it is "the subject, not the technique" that startles (116). The tensions of private and political life, the thorough pervasion of personal life by political pressures, the relentless inequality of the price paid by the two lovers involved (one of Gordimer's key structural devices to render political injustice based on race) become the local cultural material of the European novel of refined and ethical consciousness. The lesson of political inequality based on race is driven through, and in apparent contradiction to the stylish observations and reflectiveness of Jessie Stilwell. The limitations of private reflection in this context are part of the subject matter of the novel.

From the opening scenes, where white families go to view the mine dances, where old ceremonial contexts are lost and a "broken ethos" of the city is displayed, Europe and Africa are shown to have contaminated each other, to be in a process of interaction which cannot be halted. Gideon is wholly a man of the city; he has no pastoral memories or traditions to revisit. The political commitment which is the deepest layer of his being is taken carelessly from him by a white woman. The interracial affair symbolizes the unequal relationship of

Europe and South Africa, and of Europe in Africa, after colonialism and after the assertion of a racially based Afrikaner Republicanism. The cultural hybridity described at the mine dances seems to be both a gain and a loss: the "ancient instruments of Africa struck up the Colonel Bogey march" (39). "The Whites took away the African past" says Gideon at one point; at another "he had come to see his own old view of his home as as inaccurate as hers [Ann's]" (126). Ann wants authentic Africa through Gideon, "the real thing" (39), but this authenticity is a myth uncovered by the disastrous final phase of their love affair (see Griffiths).[8] Ann comes to see that perceptions in England and South Africa are different, and crucial: "...when the man in the garage looked at Gid, and I stood next to him seeing Gid at the same time, it wasn't the same person we saw..." (270). Europe and Africa are everywhere unequally mingled, with unequal results.

Jessie and Ann are two kinds of women, representing two attitudes to femininity, sexuality and women's work. Ann is " a woman without a woman's work or woman's ambition", a modern version of Schreiner's Baby-Bertie in *From Man to Man*, whereas Jessie, like Schreiner's Rebekah, is always seen as occupied either with her family, mothering, or her part-time work for a socially concerned agency. Traditional womanly strength is seen, by the end of the novel, as a fruitful ground on which political commitments can grow. This insight would later be extended in Gordimer's *My Son's Story*. Ann is described as a "new woman", and is a forerunner for a later Gordimer heroine, Hillela of *A Sport of Nature*: "in her, the kicks and snubs and the vengefulness and the hate met, complemented and merged with each other, two terrible halves of the vicious circle became whole, and healed" (92). This healing seems to be only a temporary balance, however, like the balance achieved in the central love triangle amidst African musical instruments and their indigenous sounds (50). But, as with E. M. Forster's Anglo-Indian friendship in *A Passage to India*, the country is not yet ready for women like Ann, nor for the love affair. The novel seems to hesitate, as Jessie does, between a contempt for an irresponsible Englishwoman who does not understand the realities and the costs of the South African system, and an admiration for a woman who thinks and behaves outside "the colour bar". This ambivalence is a marker of the European novelistic consciousness at work in South Africa and Jessie's problematic representation of an authorial consciousness. Jessie moves toward a more politicized awareness because her psychic amorphousness at the beach house ("The simple narrative of the beach occupied her"; "she was a plot without a theme") (195) is changed by her vicarious involvement in the affair and the suffering Gideon endures. The beach house once belonged to her stepfather, the European, Germanic Fuecht, thought by her husband to have been her biological father. This hesitation between biology and adoption in Jessie's family seems to be one of the ways in which Jessie's story moves her through a questioning of her traditional "biological purpose: sex, love and family" to a new acceptance of her own identity and relationships. She becomes a witness to the breaking of a cultural taboo and a South African law, and is changed by witnessing, as she once was when catching her mother at night emerging from a bathroom: " no longer only victim but witness of the unexplained state" (40). Ann and Jessie are drawn into the psychic exchanges of women about one man, Gideon, so that "she herself could have been Ann" (249).

The novel, so intent on illuminating the particular conditions of South African society, nevertheless relies on the highly evolved novel of individual consciousness and ethical debate. Like the quotation from Thomas Mann, *Occasion for Loving* reveals " a terrifying descent through the 'safety of middle-class trappings to the individual anarchy and ideological collapse lying at their centre" (196). Ann retrieves her marriage and escapes to Europe; Jessie is changed, though she, too, when driving through the township and its teeming improvised life, feels that the continuity of the land is not hers, nor "the authority of a legendary past" (269). Gideon, so tied by his commitment to an underground historical evolution, is left without a future.

The ideological space of the novel is "this island or mainland, in new old Africa or old new Europe" (277/8). The cultural translation of the European novel of manners and sensibility to the South African context reveals the discontinuities between form and content, and is a part of the moral judgment that is delivered. Even a happily married woman like Jessie feels her life as " a bird let into a series of cages, each one larger than the last; and each one... seeming, for a while, to be without limit, without bars" (15). The different prisons of race, class and gender are shown in complex relationship to self, houses, rooms, and identity, and daily life as " a city built on the site of a series of ruined cities" (22). The idea of a civilized love affair, even "more civilized" for flouting a local barbarism of colour prejudice, is shown to be a veneer over atavism, and the blackness of the lover, which is supposed to change nothing, changes everything in a country like the South Africa of the time. Boaz calls Gideon a "black bastard", " filthy cock" (159). Like Kurtz, his civilization is a veneer, and he falls into racial animus and disgust. The narrative of degeneracy which is a justification of segregation and black powerlessness in Millin, and is tied to unconscious sexual revulsion in Plomer and Van der Post, is critically framed in *Occasion for Loving* by an ironically presented liberalism. By showing the regression in Boaz from a liberal tolerance to racial disgust, Gordimer reveals the unconscious projective processes of European imperialism. Though Jessie is changed, her change is part of the luxury of her privacy, and her voyeurism. Her private strength at the end is at least the precondition for public involvement, but is itself built on a liberal premise of individual enlightenment and action. The novel cannot escape its own tension between liberal guilt and moral awareness: it articulates the problematic white English-speaking identity at the time of the Republic and its fraught relationship with any form of South African nationalism.

Gordimer would rework the "miscegenation novel" twice more, in *A Sport of Nature* (1989) and in *My Son's Story* (1991). The former also celebrates the opportunities of a woman whose sexuality is her path to growth and new relationships, ones that take her into a new kind of family. *My Son's Story* has a harsher lesson: that an adulterous love affair eats into the fabric of the family and political commitments. There is still a cost attached to the crossing of the racial barrier, because of the mistrust caused between comrades in a later, more polarized political environment. Habits of thought and cultural norms exceed the legal enactments that embody them (Schultze-Engler 1996).

The miscegenation novel becomes, in Gordimer's exploration of intertwined public and private realms, a vehicle for testing the social fabric of South African life and exploring the consciousness that makes up civil society in South Africa. Power is shown to reside in the nooks and crannies of private, sexual relationships as well as political organizations, and the effects combine personal and political factors. This sophisticated understanding of the workings of power, and its expression in complex narratives, extends cultural understanding of the workings of race in a racialized colony and republic, and the workings of gender across and between races in such a society. The differences between women who do "women's work" and who do not work at all, those who suffer jealousy and those for whom it is an unheard of luxury, are drawn in relation to racial policy, exclusions and privations. The laws of the country saturate the private world, but memory and contiguity of experience eventually shape a compassionate memory across racial barriers which becomes the basis of new understanding. This creation of compassionate memory is the cultural work of narrative. At the same time, as South Africa now rehearses memory and forgetting, Gordimer's *Occasion for Loving* tells us that identity and memory are multi-layered and shifting, subjectively and culturally determined. The love between Gideon and Ann, radiant for while, and measured by the depths of his dejection and loss, creates a basis for inter-racial love at the time a destructive Republic was coming into being in South Africa. This inter-racial love extends beyond the couple to a witness who stands in for a woman writer and recorder: "So long as Gideon did not remember, Jessie could not forget" (288).

Chapter Six
Novels of Colonial and Postcolonial Migrancy: Alan Paton, Peter Abrahams, Nadine Gordimer

"Awakening on Friday morning, June 20, 1913, the South African native found himself, not actually a slave, but a pariah in the land of his birth." – Sol T. Plaatje, *Native Life in South Africa*

South Africa was part of a global process of industrialization and urbanization at the turn of the nineteenth century. This affected more than one population group, with the impoverished rural Afrikaners migrating to the cities at the same time as a landless African majority, the former being distinguished from the outset by forms of government protection for their labour rights, training and general welfare in urban centres. Uneducated rural workers, like Waldo in Schreiner's *African Farm*, could work as clerks or transport riders. For Waldo these options are depicted as demeaning and unsatisfactory, and he returns to the farm, much like Alan Paton's Stephen Kumalo about seventy years later. For Africans, mine labour would become the majority occupation in the Transvaal, and the theme of the alienated rural African encountering urban culture made an early appearance in vernacular and English literature. Social upheaval and the 'Jim-comes-to-Jo-burg' theme emerged in two early Xhosa novels, *U-Nomalizo* (1918) by Enoch S. Guma and *U-Nolishwa* (1931) by Henry M. Ndawo. It was also the theme of an early novel in English by R. R. R. Dhlomo, *An African Tragedy, A Novel in English by a Zulu Writer* (1928) (Gerard 107) Dhlomo's novel establishes the idea of a tragic framework for African urbanization, and a Christianized attitude toward urban social degradation that would be replicated in Alan Paton's *Cry, the Beloved Country* in 1948.

Albert Gerard has suggested that the pattern of colonization often meant that "vernacular writers gained access to Western literature through the educational system established under European rule... the novel and Western type drama appeared to them more appropriate for conveying contemporary experience: the clash of values and the ethical and social problems arising in the newly urbanized, newly industrializing societies..." (Gerard 19). The treatment of this theme by African and white South African writers, in vernacular languages as well as English, points to a certain cultural convergence in articulating a major social upheaval. This upheaval has also been articulated by Nigerian writer Chinua Achebe, whose novels, suggests Wole Soyinka, "are not strictly works that project a social vision, being primarily concerned with evocations of actuality at points where... 'Africa was made to leave her history, her true history'" (Cabral, Gerard 87). In this sense the novels of South African urbanization and labour migration are part of a much wider African phenomenon, though 'true history' would now be a contested phrase in critical theory and historiography, which stresses narrative construction in both literature and history. Other Africanists have suggested that in the process of acculturation alienation is "the generating principle of culture, the condition of human development" (Irele, quoted by Gerard 21). Writers who emphasize he broken tribe and reify it into a changeless tragedy have not necessarily been on the side of progressive political change.

In South Africa land policy coincided with patterns of territorial segregation and enforced urbanization controlled by a myriad laws. The slavery and indentured labour of eighteenth century Dutch policy was followed by British rule (from the second occupation of 1806) where rule of law and unfree labour practices impeded progress (Crais 2). Trade and Christianity were in new alliance under the British, with links to international capital after the discovery of mineral wealth, gold and diamonds, in the last quarter of the nineteenth century.

Paton's *Cry, the Beloved Country* (1948) carries some of the ideological load of the alliance of trade and Christianity, which served to discourage independent African political organization around labour issues. Some historians trace the development of labour policy and its close relationship to pass legislation to the disintegration of Xhosa Society on the Cape eastern frontier. In 1856 the Masters and Servants

Act chained workers to their masters, and the 1857 Kaffir Pass Act and Kaffir Employment Act prohibited Xhosa from entering the colony except to work (Crais 212). According to Clifton Crais, these two Acts "helped produce a manageable working class and helped establish South Africa's modern migrant labour system" (212). Migration partly reproduced traditional social organization of the sexes, with women engaged in agriculture now remaining in the reserves in the same occupation, and the men, previously responsible for tending the cattle, migrating to work, further and further afield. Women in a rural homeland are still gathering wild spinach in July's People (1981). "But the system of migrant labour" Crais points out, "also relied on the violence of the state" (214). This state violence is differently acknowledged and incorporated in the novels of labour migration.

After World War I there was a polarization of South African society around "a clash of interest based on status and class" (Davenport 192), and the main conflicts in the nineteen-twenties were between white owners and white workers, as exhibited in the 1922 strike. The 1924 Industrial Conciliation Act restricted the use of collective bargaining to whites and coloureds only. Nevertheless, these white conflicts took their meaning from "another political struggle-that between the white community as a Whole and the African and Asian communities for political and economic control" (Davenport 175). This tension between a foregrounded class and labour struggle and the broader struggle for an African political presence is evident in Abrahams's *Mine Boy* and Paton's *Cry, the Beloved Country*.

People resisting incorporation into proletarianization could practise desertion or theft; in the cities an informal sector around illegal liquor brewing was a viable and often chosen occupation especially for urbanized women (Bonner). Stephanie in *Too Late the Phalarope* is a forerunner for Leah in Abrahams's *Mine Boy*, the full-blown "skokiaan queen", and Maisie, Xuma's friend, illustrates the alternative of domestic service. Memory, imagination, and the spread of literacy would help to contest the hegemonic alliance of a domestic oligarchy with an internationally inflected capitalist structure. Hertzog's earlier Nationalist policy of territorial segregation had been made dependent on Africans learning how to develop the reserves more effectively, and the ideological direction of Paton's narrative in

Too Late the Phalarope supports a Nationalist rationale while apparently espousing liberal tenets (Davenport 205-6).[1]

Peter Abrahams's *Mine Boy* (1946) adopts a secular stance towards the process of urbanization, though *Mine Boy* is also haunted by the countryside, towards which Xuma and Maisie journey when they visit a farm on the urban periphery, and when Xuma and the woman he loves, Eliza, walk beyond the city to the semi-rural periphery. "Xuma from the north" arrives in "Malay Camp", a generic urban Johannesburg location in which the races mix and where a fragmented and adapted culture survives in the street dances of courtship, in song and oral tales. "Daddy", an African reduced to drunken degradation, tells Xuma one of the first stories he hears, a bitter allegory about the struggle between "the custom" and "the city", in which the city always wins.

At first we see rampant street fights in which men and women define themselves in physical confrontations and the face-downs of gangsterism. Leah, the successful beer-brewer, runs her own business, looks after strays, bribes her own spies, and kills informers. She also inverts the conventional gender paradigm, taking some men as "playthings", fighting and killing men, and making the rules of the household. Survival in the city depends on being quick-witted and informed, and on criminal strategies. This daily world is not a conventionally moralized landscape, and we are shown early on that mine labour destroys health and sometimes life through miners' pthisis, and that the daily labour is regimented and deadeningly repetitive (a scene reminiscent of Coketown shows miners carting away endless vistas of yellow mine sand). Xuma falls in love with Eliza, who is a schoolteacher attracted by the ways and goods of the white world, and the story turns on the painful course of their love affair against the backdrop of Xuma's initiation into mine labour. He is inducted by an unfair test of strength by an Afrikaner boss, and at this moment symbolizes physical endurance and the strength of mining labourers. His "white man", Paddy, represents sympathetic working class whites and a European (Irish) lack of colour prejudice, the informed unionist stance of the South African Communist Party. As the narrative develops, Xuma sees that he cannot fully accept whites as friends: "more and more he saw only his own people" (102). He witnesses forms of destruction in the city, of Daddy by alcohol, of some women by sexual conflict and poverty, of Eliza by white aspirations, of himself by loneliness and labour. At the same time the city is charted in a progressive sequence of encounters and memories with different cityspaces, "rising high above its causes" (121). Xuma becomes a citizen of Malay Camp through experience and adaptation, and gradually gives up Eliza for Maisie, who accepts her own people.

The novel's epigraph, from Kipling ("But there is neither East nor West, Border, nor Breed nor Birth, / When two strong men stand face to face, / Though they come from the ends of the earth") is fulfilled at the climax of the plot, when Xuma and Paddy together defy a racial divide of allegiance after a mine accident due to white supervisors' carelessness. Though the novel's multi-racial alliance at the end suggests a humanism that Soyinka, for instance, finds too facile as a solution, it does herald the multiracial alliances that would eventually forge a successful labour movement, and would work in a subversive way against white dominated politics. Moreover, the outcome reveals that political defiance was the only way in which to contest a citizenship built on domicile without rights, a domicile we see created in the different urban spaces traversed by Xuma, of which Leah's shebeen is the centre. The masculine codes of physical fights over women and alcohol with which the novel opens are converted into masculine codes of strength used in a politically purposive way, heralding the "more purposeful black political leadership" after 1945 (Davenport 246). The fictional Xuma's career thus represents the way in which the African National Congress relied on induction of the rank and file through urban deprivation and politicization, and of the historical Congress leader Xuma's inclusion of other races (1943), centralization of the ANC, and struggle for freedom from discriminatory law and adult suffrage (Davenport 246).

In *Mine Boy* we see far more of the daily contest between police and criminal activities, the pass requirements, and the informer system on which both shebeens and police relied. By the end of the novel Maisie will be waiting for a partner facing a criminal sentence for politically inspired labour defiance. The final political conflict arises out of organic causes and problems, Xuma's experiences in Malay Camp and the mine. Xuma illustrates Abrahams's thesis, that there are three levels of living: the first is basic struggle; the second is struggle charged with social content but based on group exclusiveness; at the third the "mind takes hold of the instinct. The will casts out fear" and this is "the level of the whole man" in the "fight for light against darkness" (1953: 27). The progression toward a non-racial culture is illustrated through individual experience and character interaction.

In *Cry, the Beloved Country*, Paton's protagonist, Stephen Kumalo, is a poor, pious Zulu priest who goes to the city in quest of his lost sister, Gertrude, and son, Absalom. The novel opens in both of the first two books with invocations of the Natal countryside, and documents soil erosion and the fragmentation of the rural African populace. These descriptions tend to reify "the soil" in metaphors such as "the soil cannot keep them [the indigenous people] any more", presenting the movement of the land in tragically timeless and causeless terms. The land, the broken tribes, and the urban crime and prostitution into which Absalom and Gertrude Khumalo have fallen in economic need and despair are all presented as "sickness", as a falling away from a moral norm, not the results of specific economic, social and political motives and laws passed by a white electorate. The choric refrains on the sickness and the broken tribes do much to reinforce this effect.

The presentation of urban Africans is for the most part reliant on the stereotype of the 'agitator', and John Khumalo, the political demagogue, is presented as a corrupt foil to his brother's Christian conscience and norms. He can turn the law to his own advantage and his marital infidelity is a foregrounded concern. The African priest Msimangu, possibly based on the labour activist Msimang who later withdrew from labour struggles, advocates segregation and later withdraws into a monastery.[2] His quietism is presented as a first achievement for a black priest. Stephen Khumalo's position as a totally assimilated Christian pastor relies on righteousness and purity; his conscience and repentance are the focus of the novel, not the sufferings of his son or his sister. Absalom is described as frightened by his crime, but the death sentence is not questioned for his murder of the noblest white liberal in Johannesburg, Arthur Jarvis. Gertrude is described as an unregenerate sensualist, and so is Absalom's girlfriend: African women, unless they are married and Christian, represent original sin and troubling desire. They cannot wait to get back to the fleshpots of the city and their wicked ways.

Paton offers detailed historical events and places, and dramatizes conflicting popular South African discourses and voices. These mini-dramas of generally conservative opinion present the "native problem" as insoluble because of widespread fear, and the novel's focus on white fear invokes the concept of white colonial moral panic so well described by Doris Lessing in *The Grass is Singing* (Gardiner). The plot trajectory reinforces the emphasis on fear, because a liberalization of prison reformatory protocols (like those introduced by the historical Paton at Diepkloof reformatory) has led to a racial murder, the kind of murder often cited in support of tightening influx control and pass legislation in the cities. The positive multi-racial incidents Paton describes are always acts of individual kindness or generosity, with white people amazingly going out of their way to show solidarity with events like the bus boycott, and the African responses from Msimangu and Khumalo being overawed and grateful. This gratitude toward the white farmer benefactor, a changed Jarvis Snr, becomes a paean of thankfulness for a delivery of milk and the building of a dam in the final scenes. The novel's conclusion does suggest that a return to the valley of Ndotsheni and improved agricultural practices are the answer, though a temporary one, to the crisis of urbanization. The documents found after Arthur Jarvis's death set out the liberal principles of one who has discovered that Christianity conflicts with segregationist policy, and who advocates improved education and the settlement of native families in the cities, rather than the family separations involved in migrant labour.

Paton chooses to set this story of racial murder by a young African 'criminal' in the year of the miners' strike, which he treats very briefly. The plot structure is also a nexus of white South African concerns and anxieties about the urban African presence, and white responses to stronger pressures for adult African suffrage. A young black delinquent, the kind Paton the penologist tried to reform through greater freedom and responsibility, murders a white liberal 'son'; the murder is a result of liberalization and is also a form of parricide, as the 'criminal' impulses of the boy Khumalo are set loose upon the world and he shoots in fear of a white 'master'. Law and order are reaffirmed when Absalom is hanged for his crime, and when his father Stephen is forgiven by the white farmer, Jarvis Snr, for having fathered a murderer. Murderous impulses are thus acted out and reconciled in the new relationship of the two fathers back in the countryside, and a conservative agrarian patriarchy, slightly renovated, is reaffirmed. The city is a bad place; Johannesburg is hell (158). The fear of black rebellion, of "Africa resurgent", which Paton treats sardonically in his dramatic dialogues, is reaffirmed in the plot trajectory and the murder story. The only point at which Paton gestures towards a changed future, apart from the redeemed valley metaphor, is in his apostrophe to the African child: "Dance with the first slow steps of the dance that is for yourself... " (207).

Though the plight of urbanized Africans and the squatters is registered sympathetically, the novel's focus on forgiveness and the personal conscience is problematic. Paton's hero-worship of great South African white liberals makes him couch his resolution in terms of an individual benefactor, a rural symbol for the capitalist benefactor he appeals to in his foreword, Ernest Oppenheimer. The interlocking of capitalism and urban influx control, which could only be opposed by successful labour and political organization, is broken apart in the privileging of individual philanthropy. The novel's story of interracial murder in the city authenticates the worst fears of white South Africans: white liberals would be murdered by the ungrateful natives they were attempting to help; any liberalization and attempt at reform would backfire. African women preferred being prostitutes and beer-brewers to honest labourers in white households, and once they had become carelessly sexual soon became unregenerate, unless one caught them young. Purity of conscience is valued over survival or just opposition. Labour activists tend to be corrupt agitators, like the Communists. This convergence of white fears in the plot structure and ethical imperatives displays the construction of a bilingual white hegemony, the hegemony that would transform the policy of racial segregation into a set of ever more stringent laws after 1948.

The construction of a bilingual white nation is mirrored in Paton's glossary of terms, in which he insistently mentions that certain words in South Africa, taken from Afrikaans, are now "as fully English" words, a uniquely South African vocabulary that he is celebrating as the common linguistic emergence of a national, autonomous identity for South Africa. But this national identity was that of an all-white electorate that had spent considerable time deleting a minority African and Coloured presence from the Cape franchise, and had ended up selecting a few white representatives in Parliament for the black majority. English and Afrikaner political attitudes were hardening around a few unshakeable common principles. One of these was that if Africans were to have any rights, they should be in the distant reserves. *Cry, the Beloved Country* endorses this white consensus in its sentimental ending on a note of agricultural upliftment in Ndotsheni. The all-white state that was coming into existence is romantically conflated with the nation, and its new hybrid form of 'english'.

The male codes of the novel are patriarchal and puritanical; monogamy, after the presentation in Mhudi of its natural basis in attraction and loyalty, has hardened into a Christian code of duty which punishes sensuality. Khumalo is holier than his missionary mentors, and sometimes as tortuous in his purity as the historical Paton. The ecological focus of the novel carries a charge of nostalgic romanticism which is that of the homesick white colonial, and landscape is romanticized at the expense of any political repudiation of an unjust system based on grossly unfair land allocation. The South African presence is bifurcated into the 'good native' (Stephen Kumalo and Msimangu), who is thoroughly Christianised and grateful, and the 'bad native' (John and Absalom Khumalo) who breaks the law and takes politics into his own hands. Paton's moralized structure and his emphasis on a linguistic alliance between Afrikaans and English as the basis of common nationhood in fact announce the phase of Republicanism that had recently been cemented in the Centenary Celebrations of the Great Trek, in which he participated in 1938. Against this has to be set the mobilization of an international conscience about race relations in South Africa through the enormous international success of the novel.[3] Though in some ways Khumalo is Paton in blackface, and embodies a spirit of Christian white custodianship for the wicked lost children of the city, the haunting of the novel by inter-racial friendship forged in suffering and shared loss strikes a deep chord in South African political history.

In 1980 Nadine Gordimer would show an enforced reverse migration to an African reserve after a posited political coup in Johannesburg. In *July's People* the Smales family travel to their servant's homeland under his protection and discover the abject poverty there. By then the lifestyles of whites and Africans in the city have hardened into polarized economic opposition, and urban Africans are domestic workers and labourers only. When Maureen Smales and July eventually confront each other, when he assumes the manhood that city life and domestic service have taken from him, he speaks to her in an African language she cannot understand. And yet she understands fully what he is conveying to her: that their relationship as madam and servant has been a lie and a pretence. His assertion of his own language at that point conveys the way in which African languages in South Africa have often been separated from nationalist aspiration by the common cultural form of English, and often from personal dignity, and needed to be reunited in some way. His act of self-assertion is like that of Xuma at the end of *Mine Boy*, because it has a political and gendered dimension. *July's People* reveals the moral and economic bankruptcy of the homelands system for rural and urban South Africans, and the political interdependence of rural and urban structures. The code of Christian marriage that is Paton's moral anchorage is revealed as materially conditioned and racially condoned; when the white South African state collapses, so does the Smales' marriage. It cannot survive in the changed circumstances of the impoverished homelands. Gender codes have a material dimension, and in South Africa have been invested in a racial order.

Gordimer's *The Conservationist* (1974), haunted as it is by the trivialization and vulgarization of impulses towards country life in the city, and the haunting presence of a dead African in the "soil", draws together the implications of capitalism and its relationship with African labour, poverty and racial policy. The conservationist ending of *Cry, the Beloved Country* is pasted over conservative political impulses and fears for white security. In Gordimer's *The Conservationist* a set of ironies around capitalism, land policy and urban sexuality reveal that the alliance of white power, property and privilege has led to a more profound degradation than could have been envisaged by Stephen Kumalo in 1946. The alternative, one that would soon be historically activated by resistance politics after 1948, would be the prison sentence for political defiance that Xuma from the north faced as he returned to the scene of the miners' strike.

The Conservationist can be read as an intertextual reply to Paton's earlier fictionalization of the relationship between capitalism, urban and rural tensions, and political action, but it also, as Dennis Walder has argued, represents a formal shift in narrative poetics, coinciding with the publication of Coetzee's *Dusklands* (1974) :

> *The Conservationist* marks a crisis in the way the colonial imagination deals with the reality it perceives; a crisis that leads to the collapse of the traditional narrative relationship with society, now imagined as a mere surface, through which writer and reader fall towards a radically new form, more responsive to impersonal, psychological and historical forces which, as Gordimer comes to acknowledge, are struggling to be born (Walder 167).

The novel also shows how white novelists were finding new ways to mediate "the texture of everyday life for black people" (Walder 168). Though there are no migrations in *The Conservationist*, the novel is both postcolonial and postmodernist in its interplay of formal features, mythic structure and political documentation. The formal features of the novel, by freeing consciousness from the developmental structure of the Bildungsroman, allow richer insights into the haunting of white consciousness by the repressed black majority. The floating black body awaiting reburial represents a majority claim to social justice, lost between the myriad of apartheid laws and the loss of African traditions. It also represents the literal and existential homelessness of Africans in the city where permanent rights have been so elusive. The African farm now exists in the city as a trivialized, degraded space, but the symbolism of the eggs and children in the opening scene is an invocation to the future: " a clutch of pale freckled eggs set out before a half-circle of children" (166).

In the mid-seventies white South African novelists were creating new relationships between poststructuralism, gender and race in order to undo some of the process of "epistemic violence" that Spivak has defined as the key effect of imperialist narrative (Landry 191). In these new narrative spaces, created as a more amorphous field of signification, narrative becomes "a meta-code, a human universal on the basis of which transcultural messages about the nature of a shared reality can be transmitted" (H. White 1). These narrative shifts were in part a response to the watershed of the mid-seventies with its widespread forms of political insurrection, and a partial undoing of the colonial consciousness and its cultural control of the means of representation.

Chapter Seven
Petrified Gardens and the River of Life: Versions of Anti-pastoral

> "He would clear the rubble from the mouth of the shaft, he would lower it down the shaft deep into the earth, and when he brought it up there would be water in the bowl of the spoon; and in that way he would say, one can live." – J.M. Coetzee, *The Life and Times of Michal K*.

Postcolonial critics and theorists have been grappling with the problem of "the agency of the oppressed" (Crais 2) after poststructuralism, the recognition of white bias and narrative itself in historiography, and the appropriation of Third World problems and perspectives by First World commentators. Another belated recognition has been that colonizers are as affected as the colonized, certainly in terms of psychological deformation, though not of economic benefit. South African fiction in the second half of the twentieth century has been preoccupied with the emotional effect of apartheid as an organized system of labour control, disenfranchisement and daily surveillance (Crais 4). Nadine Gordimer has suggested that this has marked off the terrain of South African literature in an idiosyncratic way, that the set of problems dealt with by novelists has been generated by artificial racial structures and legislation, and that a "true" (i.e. unitary) culture could only come into being after the fall of apartheid: " We have created our own sense of sin and our own sense of tragedy" (Gordimer 1961) .

In recent postcolonial critique, this view of South Africa and cultures is contested. National narrative is "never pure or holistic but always constituted in a process of substitution, displacement or projection" (Bhabha, quoted ECW 205). This view has displaced a Manichean view of culture derived directly from the political segregation within South Africa. Many critics have pointed out that white South Africans have suffered the loneliness of a powerful minority, and that a vibrant life could only be lived in an African township. Different critical standards have operated within South Africa (with demands for political address and social realism) and outside, whether in the South African diaspora or in the theoretical debates generated in the wake of poststructuralism (with demands for more formal complexity than social realism and a recognition of the prior politicization of language and genre).

J. M. Coetzee has been particularly adamant in his claim that the novel should not attempt to replicate historical discourse, that its mode of operation and epistemology are different, that storytelling generates activities and responses that should not too readily be conflated with other forms of knowledge and discourse. He has argued that the novel of character belongs to a dead bourgeois world, that language has constitutive power, and subjectivity is generated in the process of narration. His novels have sought to address nationalist structures in South Africa by constructing an echo-chamber in which some of the regional specifics are dissolved, so that South African involvement in global structures of colonialism, dependency and racialism is revealed through narrative. Because his novels lay bare a mythological and psychological substructure they have revealed forms of social and political interdependence: of capitalism and racism, of nationalism and capitalism, of masters and servants, of urban and rural structures. As development theorists have argued, "nationalism... is the familiar locus of legitimating social myths in the modern period and... nationalist sentiment a functional requisite of the establishment of autonomous capitalisms within the world economy" (Preston 14). Though the twentieth century saw the rise of Afrikaner nationalism and the concurrent institutionalization of apartheid (Gerard 106), there was also a growing sense of political resistance, triggered in part by African nationalist sentiment and a wealth of oppositional strategies but also by the imaginative responses of literature, which offers " a continuing process of self-apprehension" (Soyinka xi). As Stefano Harney has pointed out in the context of Caribbean nationalism, there has often been a "tension between the idea of a nation as an independent unfettered political whole and the idea of a nation as a people"

(10). Because Afrikaner nationalism asserted itself with defensive and offensive racist legislation, opposition involved a growing sense of humanist affirmation and the need for multi-racial collaboration, despite the more polarized phase of Black consciousness in the sixties and seventies. As Kenneth Parker has argued, South Africa has also been "an interdependent, multi-racial society" (xi).

One strand within the weave of the South African novel as it responded to the surrounding social matrix has been that of "Karoo fabulation', fiction locating itself within the heartland of the semi-arid Karoo in the Cape Colony, a scene of isolated sheep and cattle farming where the ideological outlines of a subsequent South African white-controlled state and the crass master-servant hierarchy could be observed in all its harshness. Much of this harshness – an embattled, ignorant, authoritarian order – can be seen in Schreiner's African Farm, which Coetzee has called an "anti-pastoral" in its lack of human community and dystopic vision. Schreiner's farm is "a figure in the service of her critique of colonial culture" (1988: 66). He has also argued that Pauline Smith's pastoralism is transplanted from the semi-aristocratic order of the British novel, that it is a "regional answer" to the South African complex, in its benign patriarchy and "selective vision of precapitalist social life" (1988: 72).

Although Coetzee has argued that there is no Edenic myth in South African literature, only the Israelite one which validates the white tribe of Afrikaners, Smith locates the "river of life" in the garden at the Harmonie homestead in the Little Karoo, in the protected world of childhood, and even Schreiner's drought-stricken farm effloresces in the last section of the narrative when the main characters return to tell their stories, and Lyndall's sacrificial death regenerates the rivers and vegetation. The farm novel seems to be haunted by a vision of a more harmonious community which never quite arrives.

Coetzee has remarked on the South African novelist's over-preoccupation with questions of power. Modern South African novelists have found the Karoo farm a convenient fictional locus to allegorize power relations, distortions of humanity in the ruthless master-servant relationship and extortionist labour policy in the society at large.

Dan Jacobson's *A Dance in the Sun* (1956) builds on Schreiner's portrait of unflinching sun, exacerbated tyrannies and collusive power, and begins to suggest the complicity and hopelessness of white liberalism to provide an answer to the intractable power problems between Afrikaner and African. Two Jewish students are sidetracked from their travels through the Karoo to stay briefly at a Gothic farmhouse where they become unwilling witnesses to the incestuous relationships between an English South African farmer, Fletcher, his Afrikaans wife, her brother, Nasie (Nation) Louw, and an African servant, Joseph, whose sister has been impregnated by Nasie prior to her disappearance. The Jewish students act as detectives with a conscience, and try to extract Joseph's story of his wanderings about the country to track down his sister and child. Their attempts at structuring a coherent narrative parallel Joseph's attempt to discover his sister's story and the causes of her flight. Joseph's patience, and his Christian name, suggest the scapegoating of the black servant family on the farm, representing an African majority whose humanity has been insulted and whose family life has been disrupted but who wait patiently at the gate for history to turn, for the truth to be revealed.

The white farming family are presented as frustrated in their impulses toward connection, affection, and culture, as a parody of a gentlemanly colonial order. The Afrikaner's sexual connection with the African woman servant allegorizes the making and the hiding of the parallel mixed-race population, sexually connected in secrecy but not part of the literate culture which puts out the dominant myths. The harshness to and humiliation of Joseph invites a nemesis which is pending by the end of the novel.

Jacobson's novel thus begins to explore the problem of the replication of the basic power structure within white discourse, and, by enclosing Joseph's patient search for his sister and her child and his account of that search within the larger 'liberal' narrative, he offers a symbolic reading of the problems of white authorship and ethical responsibility. Jacobson's familiarity with Schreiner's novel allows him to rework the farmhouse as South African allegorical scenario, to suggest the destruction of the settler enterprise by the destructive passions of Nasie Louw, who does his best to wreck the farmhouse, and who has been excluded from the farm by his sister's marriage to an Englishman. A shared bilingual white state has begun to draw down the vengeance of a more conservative Afrikaner, the rural Afrikaner who claimed a sexual right to African women servants. Jacobson draws on the mode of the suspense novel, the murder mystery, to suggest that Afrikanerdom has a guilty secret at the heart of its ideological structure which may one day subvert its power completely.

J. M. Coetzee's *In the Heart of the Country* (1977) is a more complex allegory in that, as one critic has remarked, there is no steady referentiality for signifiers within the narrative. In fact this referentiality is subverted (Zamora 45). Indeterminacy is foregrounded by the narrative method which leaves the reader with radical doubts about the truth status of events described, often multiple descriptions of key scenes, and the doubts suggested about the sanity and reliability of the speaker of a sectioned dramatic monologue, Magda (an anagram of the Afrikaans word "maagd", virgin). *In the Heart of the Country* is constructed as a woman's voice speaking out of the mythological centre of white rural hegemony on "Agterplaas" (the retrogressive farm of the hinterland) . Hendrik, the main 'Coloured' or 'Hottentot' servant, comes from the location called Armoede (poverty). The narrative, as bleak and ugly as the farm, concerns Magda's fantasy life, in which she dreams of murdering her authoritarian father after he has brought a second wife back to the farm (who may or may not be Klein-Anna, Hendrik's new wife, who arrives in a sequentially later scene, and whom her father seduces, or rapes). She also dreams of being raped by Hendrik in his vengeance against her and her father, or she is raped by him. The truth status of these central and repeated events is always in question. There is a graphic dwelling on the body and bodily processes: excretion, cruelty, wounds, sexuality, the ugliness of Magda's flesh, her unappealing womanhood. She constantly describes herself in terms of lack and emptiness, as vacancy, as a voice calling out and speaking without response and reciprocity, as being unable to get beyond the barriers and circumscription of language in order to communicate with the farm servants, though she invites them to live in the farmhouse after burying her father.

Magda's symbolic revenge is followed by the material demands of the servants, who are partly dependent on a cash economy, and want to be paid for their labour. The subordinate status of patriarchal daughters is shown up by the turn of events: Magda cannot access the bank funds, and does not know about taxes and farm activities, which have always been men's work. Her tasks have been to serve her father, manage the domestic servants, run the bath, polish his boots, and organize meals. Presumably her acts of vengeance against her father are part of an unresolved incestuous love and also what Coetzee has called "the castrating urge behind South African baasskap", the humiliation of the weak by the strong (Gallagher 1991: 92). This impulse cuts several ways on the farm, depending on who wields the power. An incestuous sharing of beds and tracking of people about the farm suggests the arrogation of women as chattels by the white farmer, and the vengeful response of the male servant in turn. The 'farm' has become, or always was, the site of an ambiguous and starved fantasy life, the site of repression, with language repeatedly imaging deferred desire, affection, and communication.

Some critics have read *In the Heart of the Country* as a subversion of Afrikaner nationalist myths concerning women as the emblems of purity, martyrdom and motherhood. A starved and ugly white virgin in the rural hinterland certainly offers "a new history of Afrikaner consciousness" and an embittered view of racial and sexual politics on the farm (Gallagher 94). Magda turns in the vortex created by the unequal interlocking of patriarchal and racial power, and is handed on to her 'groom', Hendrik, because she acts against her all-powerful father. She is presented as trapped within the language of hierarchy and domination; though she would like "words of true exchange" (101) she can only speak the "father-tongue" of domination. It is also western literacy that confines her within whiteness and vacancy: "My learning has the reek of print, not the resonance of the full human voice telling its stories" (47). Baulked in all her desires for connectedness, she at one point comes to rest in a fantasy in which she inhabits Klein-Anna's brown skin and body, in an image of fusion and wholeness.

The risk taken by such an extreme anti-pastoral are that the location of a frustrated voice outside history, with the "castaways of history", and "God's forgotten" places the Afrikaner outside the historical process. The postmodernist devices underline this effect: there is no certainty about arrivals and departures, deaths and births here. Historical process is abrogated to give the vacancy at the heart of the country and its ugly authoritarian and incestuous secrets some space to speak their names. But by making this voice belong to a frustrated spinster on the edge of craziness Coetzee risks equating women's anatomy with a lack of 'true" language , and 'true' sexuality. At one point Magda declares that " anatomy is destiny", thus subverting the political reading of her own narrative, that it is the social construction of gender difference within a racialized patriarchy that has dispossessed her. If she is seen with pathos, as the daughter of "God's forgotten", then the Afrikaners, too, are absolved as historical actors, are pathetic victims. It is her fate to die on a barbarous frontier "in the petrified garden" (119), but the deterministic course of her fate has been invented by a male author. *In the Heart of the Country* can be seen as a replication, from within, of the destructive course of Afrikaner Nationalist mythology, and its date, 1977, marks it as a fictive equivalent of the death-knell that sounded in the 1976 insurrections for the proponents of racial segregation and cultural isolation.

The burden of gender ideology is less easy to read: Magda is given a voice to tell her unhappy story, and character is not abolished even in a postmodern dramatic monologue, but revealed: farm spinsters want to be raped by Coloured servants; Coloured servants will usually oblige. While the arrogation of farm servant women by white farmers has much historical validation in South Africa, inter-racial rape of white women does not. Such violence has normally occurred within overcrowded black townships. Magda seems to embody the Lacanian thesis that access to language marks permanent dispossession for women, and all they can do is rage and fantasize revenge. Yet Magda is also "a heroine of consciousness" who would like to be "the median between contraries" (119). The extent to which sexuality and the body, pleasure and humanism have been subordinated or totally occluded by the politics of race and authority in South Africa marks *In the Heart of the Country* as an ambiguous text within Karoo fabulation, and the politics of race and gender. Yet the date of its publication also draws a causal relationship between the bleakness of racial origins, racial policy, and violent political consequences.

As the whole narrative can be said to be a translation from Afrikaans into English, not just the dialogue originally written in Afrikaans, it also stands on a frontier of cultural translation between Afrikaners and English-speakers, between South Africa and an international audience with whom it has colonial parallels and discoordinates. As Coetzee has indicated in *White Writing*, after discussing the European paradigms of travel literature, there may be "radical differences of material culture between two societies, even, one might speculate, radical differences of cultural outlook" (42-3). The question is whether, in using an ugly, frustrated spinster daughter on a South African farm to render the psychic underlife of a rural racist order, Coetzee has not reproduced a patriarchal, even misogynist view of women. Similarly, the abstract, dehumanized texture of his early fiction partly reproduces the dehumanization of the segregationist system.

In *The Life and Times of Michael K* (1983) a different version of Karoo fabulation is offered, and a complex reworking of the story of a return to the mythical heartland of the Karoo farm. Like Magda, Michael K is a figure of powerlessness, a simpleton on the edge of sanity whose story has always seemed "all wrong", "a story with a hole in it" (150). The Coloured son of a domestic servant who dies after he has trundled her in his wheelbarrow as far as Stellenbosch, Michael K could well be the son of Magda and Hendrik, if Magda had been a domestic servant, given that the name Anna again predominates, but the narrative is delivered at a point of generality that allows some of the aspects of all peasantries to be embodied in Michael's story. He has been a gardener at the Cape, like the first Dutch East India gardener, Hendrik Boom; he enjoys idleness, like the despised Hottentots; he resists incorporation into servitude on the farm he finally locates as his mother's possible ancestral home; he tries to resist forms of urban labour which have now become wartime conscription, as there is a war on whose point has been lost and whose sides are perhaps becoming interchangeable. He has grown up in an orphanage where punishment predominated, and has a harelip that marks him as a basic creature close to the earth, not given to much speech at all, and not wanting a medical correction into normality either, for the South African norm has become permanent civil war. His physical body is an allegorical site and a material object. Michael K is also a gardener who tries to keep the idea of gardening alive at a time of war and surveillance. Though he is at one point identified as 'Coloured', but only when institutionalized, he also embodies the spirit of African resistance to labour incorporation and proletarianization, and the mass exodus from the poisoned city resembles the original exodus from the countryside after the effects of the 1913 Land Act described by Sol Plaatje. His mother's desire to return to her vaguely remembered Karoo home resembles the story of Allie in Pauline Smith's story "Desolation", and the combination of humour and material detail in Michael's makeshift attempts to mobilize his mother for her last journey are the more moving for being so physically rendered. Michael, as irreducible man and peasant, is always struggling with the material world of objects, and this materiality comes to embody a quest for freedom, the freedom to exist at all outside institutional walls, prisons, hospitals, labour camps, cities, places of resettlement and rehabilitation.

Michael's search for free, unoccupied land and a place to plant seeds becomes not a search for the unvisited past but for the future, as he carries his plant seeds with him. Or rather, his visit to the dam on the abandoned farm, and his rural experiments there produce the seeds that he tries to take back to the city. Burying his mother's ashes on the farm begins "his life as a cultivator" (78). He enacts a crucial transition in human and Southern African development, that from nomad to cultivator. The impossibility of his quest indicates that the South African state has sown the dragon's teeth that now spring up everywhere in the violence of war and the structural violence of police and bureaucracy. The state has become coterminous with the land, so that he has to bury himself close to the earth in makeshift hideouts. His body is starved and maltreated; his minimal possessions are often at risk; he is exploited in camps and sexually humiliated by women. He is a misfit, escapee, and prisoner at different times in the narrative. In Part II of the novel, narrated by a medical officer, Michael becomes the object of western theory and philosophy, and of liberal understanding. He resists these processes as well, and Part II allows Coetzee to incorporate into the narrative a critique of those Western paradigms which judge and interpret the different, specific and indigenous processes of 'other' cultures in their own terms. Michael's 'otherness' becomes a sign of his resistance to dominant sign-systems.

Michael K rewrites the terms of "the isolationist romance of the return to the family farm" (Coetzee 1988: 3) so that Michael can represent the spirit of collective resistance to incorporation within an unjust political system, as irreducible human unit. The involuntary nature of the labour he is forced into evokes "the spectacle of native labour" and its "scandalous force" (1988: 11). He avoids private property and travels on foot with his makeshift vehicles; he lives within a subsistence economy; he has to enact many returns and seek the lowest level of life to avoid surveillance. His travels between country and city, and his picaresque adventures in both, counter traditions of the 'sublime' in landscape art and literature, and any linear narrative of social evolution and progress. His position on a hilltop on the Karoo farm at one point parodies the speculative topography of European landscape art and indicates the true owner of the farm, the peasant cultivator. A peasant culture is inscribed in the Karoo which is not that of a conservative, static, racially exclusive Afrikaner order. In offering Michael K's story as a partial redemption, the story of a man who wants to eat only "the bread of freedom", Coetzee allies himself with the tradition of the 'plaasroman' in Afrikaans: "turning from the comprehensive prospect of colonial pictorial art linked to conquest and domination to a humbler homegrown art of closely rendered particulars, grounded on love and intimacy with the land as soil" (Sole 1988:167). When Michael K finally reaches, again, the old pump on the abandoned farm, there is a gesture toward a possible future after a struggle concerned only with survival, in "the lifegiving underground water of Africa" (167).

Coetzee's metafictions involve the readers in constitutive cultural acts, and a continuing process of decoding and interpretation. As Chris Gittings suggests, narratives that foreground the "making of story" are especially valuable when cultural production is heavily invested in a political hegemony, as "they provide readers with an opportunity to recognize their own participation in cultural production" (1995: 152). Metafiction, as Linda Hutcheon has remarked, is also a predominant device "to translate an ancestral past into a narrative present, thereby creating personal and cultural identities" (Gittings 152). Acts of cultural and linguistic translation, in these texts, have a "transformative element" in bridging gaps between incommensurable systems, and offer an enabling understanding of "the dynamics of our imperialism" (Gittings 152-3). In terms of readership, though, there is a continuum between Coetzee's fictional modality and his intellectual reception. The value of his texts for reconstituting cultural identity lies in the enabling transaction readers make with voices and presences that have been deauthorized in Southern African history. At the same time the narrative control over these invented voices is called into question by deconstructive devices, confirming Dorothy Seaton's thesis that postcoloniality is not simply counterdiscursive but deconstructive (Seaton 1991). The deconstructive embraces "the endless strangeness of both land and discourse, interrogating the very capacity of discourse to constitute the land" (Seaton 1991: 77). This deconstructive turn, the foregrounding of process, is part of a politics of narrative that pre-empts the problem of narrative appropriation: of Magda's 'voice' by a male author, of Michael K's 'voice" by a white author. Versions of history, and of the future, are endlessly reconstructed within story-telling and the critical readings that keep stories and characters alive in imagination and intellect. Such processes, as Peter Abrahams argues, keep "democracy on trial in the plural societies today" (1953: 219).

Chapter Eight
Re-reading Resistance:
La Guma, Serote, Sepamla

"There was no news; you had to be contented with history." – La Guma, *In the Fog of the Season's End*

"...the children had gathered in the sunlit yard." – *La Guma, In the Fog of the Season's End*

"I fly I ride I cycle
in big and small cities
me."

– Mongane Serote

The novels of resistance written during the sixties and seventies in South Africa were responding to the crisis initiated on the 21st March 1960, with the Sharpeville anti-pass demonstrations, in which police fire killed at least 69 and injured far more, and the subsequent banning of the African National Congress and the Pan-Africanist Congress. A new phase of political history had begun, in which non-violent resistance was replaced with acts of sabotage, the recruiting of young people for military training abroad, and more deliberate and massive attempts at the creation of a political consciousness among black workers in the city and the country. The non-racial nationalism of the ANC, which was "a movement to win democratic rights for Africans" and thus reconstitute the nation, began to give way to the Black Power nationalism that became a "major ideological force" in the 1970s (Gerhart 13). In the development of black resistance fiction, a broader socio-political movement is evident, what Gail Gerhart calls "the history of postwar African thought... a protracted process of tearing loose from liberalism as a worldview" (16). In this process, certain positive cultural aims were envisaged. The movement aimed to build morale, and foster political consciousness "an understanding by individuals of their relationship to their society and... of how the parts of their society function in relation to one another" (Gerhart 18).

A related aim was to create solidarity, a sense of a common position and common interests "reorienting African ethical perspectives to reconcile moral rectitude with radical African political goals" (Gerhart 18). As all of the key political leaders were detained during the early sixties or had escaped over the border, political opposition went "underground" and these novels depict the nature of that underground struggle, a clandestine movement either in secrecy and fear of surveillance, or in prison itself. Literature became a weapon in a wider cultural and ideological struggle, to articulate social circumstances and contexts for African life, common grievances and inequities, and possible remedies. Whereas the ANC has defined the nation as "the multiracial community of all people born in South Africa" (Gerhart 12), Black Power nationalism "emphasized racially exclusive strategies for the overthrow of white domination" (Gerhart 3). Though both strands of nationalism are evident in these novels, the latter is much stronger during the polarized decades of the sixties and seventies, and solidarity between ethnic groups – African, Coloured, and Asian – was emphasized rather than interracial friendship. The overriding of tribal difference, especially in the urban melting-pots of slums and major cities, becomes a factor in social depiction and ideological intent.

In this construction of political understanding and solidarity, fiction became part of a wider attempt to counter the workings of apartheid ideology, especially in its post-Republican form, in which the police state, wide powers of surveillance, detention without trial, and the social engineering of Bantustan policy aimed to offer Africans only parochial citizenship and token power. The term 'terrorism' was given a wide interpretation and preventive detention, brutal interrogations, and deaths in custody became apparently permanent features of the police state ushered in by Prime Minister B. J. Vorster (1966 – 1978), earlier, ironically but appropriately, Minister of Justice. From 1963 to 1971, 22 black South Africans died in detention, and 21 more in the 21 months after March 1976. Steven Biko, the Black consciousness and student leader, and a focal point of gathering political anger, was the 40th black South African to die in police custody under detention without trial laws on the 12th September 1977. The number of people in detention between April 1976 and October 1977, the peak of the Soweto-inspired 'riots', increased by 900%. The social engineering in which relocations of massive numbers of people became common was part of a policy designed to keep the Africans out of a common political forum and to render them 'temporary sojourners' in the cities. In 1963 and 1970 legislation made all Africans citizens of the Bantustans or 'homelands' (created out of the reserves of the 1913 and 1936 Land Acts), translating them into foreigners in 86% of the country, irrespective of place of birth (Kane-Berman 93).[1] Having been made refugees from the countryside, they were now non-citizens and sojourners in the towns. There was also an attempt to reverse the flow of Africans to the cities, often fixing on the disabled, women or the unemployed as the beneficiaries of this policy: 465,000 Africans were endorsed out of the 23 major towns between 1956 and 1963 (Kane-Berman 75). Often these deportees were conscripted into labour camps if they chose not to be handed over to the police. These historical trends and policies are the political realities that underpin the generic camps and mythological journeying of Michael K and his co-travellers between country and city, and the social problems depicted in black resistance fiction.

The rewriting of history by the Nationalist government, a retroactive and unilateral superimposition of a tribal citizenship, was also meant to discourage political effectiveness, differentiating along ethnic and tribal lines, whereas urbanization had loosened ties with pre-industrial culture and promoted cultural integration, partly through a common subjection to discriminatory laws and daily harassment by police and bureaucracy. Even by 1953, as Peter Abrahams records in *Return to Goli*, there was " an urban, completely Westernized Black community in the Union" and "a Black culture of the cities" (159). He describes this community as in some ways more European than the Afrikaners: "The tribal content of this culture is subconscious, what the people carry with them of their tribal past. But their conscious orientation is away from the tribe and to the new, semi-universal cultural forms of the cities" (159). The largely student-inspired ideology of Black Consciousness was a response to this political climate of oppression through internal division, and to a growing urban sophistication among young educated urban Africans. Mafika Gwala describes Black Consciousness as a united front approach by students "a movement toward Black solidarity and against white racism and capitalist exploitation" (Gwala 90). It proved a powerful tool in "reactivating a consciousness of resistance" (90). Robert Fatton argues that Black Consciousness in South Africa was "a synthesis of class awareness and black cultural assertiveness" (Fatton 56), so that "class as well as race occupied a privileged position in the Black Consciousness movement analysis of the South African social formation" (Fatton 77). Novels by Black South Africans in these decades play a role in a wider "historical contestation between integration and black identity" (Gwala 91). Differences in setting and atmosphere between the Cape Town novels of La Guma and the Transvaal township novels of Serote, Sepamla and Tlali are partly the effect of "the marriage between English and Afrikaner capital" which "divided South Africa into economic regions" (Gwala 94). In sum:

> Though Black Consciousness lacked a consistent ideological basis, it did stimulate thinking of a more defined nature about the black man's struggle in South Africa, thus correcting the political imbalance left by the banning of the ANC and PAC. The sense of national expectancy had returned (Gwala 94).

La Guma's depiction of slum and city life in Cape Town, Serote's Alexandra township, and Sepamla's Wattville and Soweto bear out these observations. La Guma's use of dreamscapes under torture which reawaken traditional warrior images of courage and battle show how the subconscious tribal past could be put to literary use in *In the Fog Of the Season's End*. In *Time of the Butcherbird*, a novel dealing with rural infiltration and resistance to resettlement, the San presence and tradition is remembered, and a figure reminiscent of Plaatje's Mhudi, a woman leader, Mma-Tau, the she-lion, plays a key role in encouraging the village to object to relocation. *In the Fog of the Season's End* shows how a deeper connection with the city is forged by the pain of opposing tyranny and exploitation. The poetics of blood, given a conservative ideological direction by writers like Millin, is now given oppositional, sacrificial meaning: "...his blood had dripped into the hard grey surface of a city sidewalk, and it was as if it had taken root and held him there" (133).

The sixties and seventies also saw the spread of industrialization and secondary industry, so that mining labour became part of cultural memory as the early foundation of migration and urbanization. The number of Africans in manufacturing had doubled from 151,889 in 1939/40 to 369,055 in 1949/50. Elias Tekwane, one of the main figures in La Guma's *In the Fog of the Season's End,* has had a rural childhood, but his father has been killed in a mining accident, "buried deeper than any of his ancestors" (73) and becomes part of the deep memory of the text. Generations of urban labour had evolved, and generational conflict, foregrounded in the student-led demonstrations and leadership of the seventies, is part of the thematics of these novels of resistance, as well as a structural principle. In Serote's *To Every Birth Its Blood* the structure of the novel turns on a shift in generation as well as narrative point of view, as the main story passes from Tsi, a jazz-loving Alexandra township dweller, to his politically committed nephew, Oupa, in Part II.[2] Sepamla's *Third Generation* makes the generational debate part of the title as well as the plot, in which the "Third Generation", a revolutionary group, give Lifa's mother the task of transporting military recruits, for which she is imprisoned and tortured. A younger generation's discontent with either the submissive Christianity or the drunken defeat of their elders formed a central part of the motivation and debate in the Soweto revolt of the mid-seventies.

Gail Gerhart dates the emergence of black power nationalism from the ANC Youth League and the leadership of Anton Lembede in 1944, which stressed the use of the past to create the future, and a conversion from tribalism to African nationalism (Gerhart 51). Both of these ideological currents are evident in resistance fiction, which seeks to show discrimination while building an awareness of solidarity. As Mamdani has argued in his portrayal of "the bifurcated state", "ethnicity is both a form of cultural control over natives and the form of revolt against it" (24). The interethnic divide, he argues, is the effect of a larger split, also politically enforced, between town and country (24). This is particularly true of South Africa, with its system of controlled labour and influx control. John Kane-Berman argues that: "the politics of land ownership and influx control and the politics of the franchise are so closely linked that they amount to virtually the same thing" (91). In the construction of forms of knowledge, information, and solidarity by the novels of black resistance, these novels counter the enormous balkanisation and silencing effected in these decades of intensified conflict, raise individuals to representative levels, and create a sense of a collective and unstoppable historical movement toward victory. The depiction of daily and solitary suffering, and political martyrdom, is a part of this process.

Alex la Guma is a key figure in the development of this tradition, with his direct involvement in politics and his arrest during the Treason Trials in 1956 and his complex, substantial oeuvre. His stays in prison enabled him to depict prison life as a shadow country, another form of underground life, "the country behind the coastline of laws and regulations and labyrinthine legislation" (*The Stone Country* 81). A number of fictional techniques emerge as key strategies to build solidarity and collective awareness in resistance novels: the portrayal of the individual as constricted by a social environment; showing connections between individuals and emphasizing their interchangeability or intersubjectivity; alternating the lifestories of comrades of different ethnicities and backgrounds, such as Beukes and Tekwane in *Fog*; narrative structures that create links and continuity; imagery linking forms of underground activity (mining, prison, and covert political organization), present and past; the personification of 'the movement' itself, as the wind, as a tree with many roots, as manifold and multiple.

In La Guma's early novella, *A Walk in the Night*, he depicts a "whirlpool world of poverty, petty crime and violence" (4) in Cape Town's District Six. Michael Adonis, sacked from his job by a white boss, nurses his rage and kills a drunken old Irishman in his slum tenement. A brutal white policeman, Raalt, simmering with anger at his unfaithful wife, carelessly arrests and kills the wrong man, Willieboy, who dies in agony in a police van, remembering a childhood world of violence and abuse while the policeman chats in a nearby store. Michael Wade, in a sensitive and detailed account of this tense novella, suggests that the surface naturalism can simply encode monotony, but that the "metaphysical continuity" between Adonis and Willieboy is one sign of the presence of grace (172). The death of "the wrong man" becomes "a random sacrifice" (172), and the purpose and method of this work are aesthetic, not political. The political current is located in "somewhat simplistic politico-moral truisms" (191).

The "mistaken identity" situation can be given a political reading, however, in that both men are products of the grim socio-economic conditions so graphically rendered in the novella. The epigraph and the old Shakespearean actor both refer us to *Hamlet*: Michael Adonis kills his white 'boss' / authority figure by proxy in killing the old actor; he is punished by proxy when Willieboy dies in his stead, the victim of family abuse and state violence and neglect, personified in Raalt. The convergence of traumatic family memory at the moment of physical suffering after the shooting by the policeman suggests links between state control and the family effects of economic deprivation. A potential squabble between another slum couple, Franky and Grace Lorenzo, is averted by a moment of tenderness, and at the end of the story one character is walking toward the sea and rocks, while the pregnant Grace "feels the knot of life within her" (84). This birth image, anticipating the end of Serote's *To Every Birth Its Blood*, suggests that something has been healed by the narrative exchanges of proxy murder and proxy scapegoating. The interchangeability of Willieboy and Adonis makes a political point about the role and political causes of the social environment, and the criminal act of murder arises from an animosity toward a white boss with great power. Economics and racial policy, and their behavioural effects, are shown as inseparable, which they certainly have been in South Africa. This technique is used more subtly, and reinforced by structure, in *Fog of the Season's End* where a Prologue shows us an unidentified man brutally taken into custody and awaiting interrogation. Only towards the end of the novel do we learn that the detainee is not Beukes, but Elias Tekwane, his comrade. TekWane is murdered by police in the penultimate chapter; in the final scene, when Beukes waits for three men to arrive for transport over the border, 'Paul' is missing until Isaac, another member of the movement, arrives, and becomes 'Paul'. The assumed names, and the anonymity of the police detainee throughout most of the narrative, make the same point. In the struggle for freedom and democracy, individuality had in a sense to be yielded up: "...while there is a soul in jail, I am not free" (epigraph to *The Stone Country*). This is also one of the effects of references to "the Movement", not to a specific historical organization.

In *The Stone Country* there is also an important structural link between two men, George Adams, the political prisoner, and the Casbah Kid, the young criminal from the slums. Casbah awaits a death sentence for murder, and commits another murder while in prison, of "Butcherboy", the prison bully. The ordinary prisoners protect George from the bully; they see his importance in playing a role which might change the World they are forced to inhabit, of radical deprivation. Within the narrative there is a brief narrative, as an oral folktale, of a typical murder committed in sexual jealousy and rage. This 'common' murder story interrupts the story of the murder of "Butcherboy" and its consequences in jail, with the identity of the killer, Casbah Kid, being hidden by the group of henchmen. Yet Casbah still awaits his death sentence, and at the end of the story he is sent off to travel to his death, while George is remanded to another section. Before he leaves, Casbah tells the story of his father, hanged for the murder of his mother. In his story, he has been flung against a wall and left for dead; his brutalized mother crawls over and puts a knife in her husband's hand, then plunges it into her own throat. Casbah does not reveal this story to the police, so his father is hanged for murder. "Is this story true?" asks Adams, but Casbah does not reply. This destabilizing of his story indicts endemic conditions rather than individual cases. Does it matter if his mother's death was a suicide or a murder? The two have become almost synonymous in the degradation of their lives.

Yet Casbah seems almost pleased to be following in his father's footsteps, and is fatalistic. There is a systematic abuse of power rather than individual guilt or innocence, and at the end Casbah is called a "prisoner of war". The larger structural relations of South African society have been like those of a civil war; Coetzee's *Michael K* makes the same point. In another ironic thread of the narrative, an escape is planned by three men, but only the most reluctant one, Koppe ('Heads') who has to be forced out of the cell, actually makes it over the wall. Those who initiated resistance have not always been among the beneficiaries.

La Guma's *In the Fog of the Season's End* is a powerful indictment of a burgeoning system of racial oppression, a police state, the ruthless extermination of political activists, and the forces gathering against the system, "another dimension of terror" (3). The battering in jail is contrasted with a quiet scene in the Cape Town gardens, and a flashback to a scene in the Museum against a frieze of San figures, "the still figures of the first people" (17). Many of the political grievances are represented: Bantu education, unequal pay and compensation, forced evictions, police checks, random sexual humiliation when Elias applies for a pass, the invisibility of black urban messengers, forms of labour in town and country, the destitution and ignorance in the rural areas. This creation of a political consciousness is shown between characters, for instance in the conversation between Beukes and a domestic worker in the park, and is also a function of the text in relation to its readers. The links between Beukes and Tekwane are forged in alternating narratives and meetings and memories, until Tekwane dies in jail and Beukes continues their plans in the final chapter. The historical reach back into Southern African prehistory is projected into the future in metaphors of the movement: for instance, in an extended analogy with boxing, "The Movement writhed under the terror, bleeding" (48/49). The Sharpeville massacre makes up a key chapter in which the victims include representative people: Washerwoman, Messenger, Outlaw and Child, who set off in the morning and whose deaths are formally described at the end of the day, when rain and blood mingle. The anonymous fighter in the movement has become "a voice in a massed choir" (107). Images taken from the funfair, the circus, gangster movies, popular music and dance anchor politics in an everyday culture of ordinary people, where people meet, fall in love, and separate to undertake political work.

The depiction of factory work in the Cape, and the whole context of the novel, tend to support Martin Legassick's thesis that the spread of secondary industry was not a liberalizing force but one which entrenched apartheid and white privilege (Davenport 374).[3] This point is explicitly made when Beukes, wounded in the arm by gunfire, struggles with his wound across the wall from a white garden party where characters flirt and converse. The political lessons Elias learns are crisply articulated: "...we are not only humbled as Blacks, but also as workers; our blackness is only a pretext" (131). The historical density of La Guma's fictional world is sustained by the architectonic strength of his structured narratives; Cape Town slum characters become "characters in some obscurely metaphysical play" (*Fog* 61). La Guma takes the social realism of Graham Greene, including the focus on gangsterland and depravity, and turns it to vivid ideological use. The gathering of the power of resistance in the semi-genteel shabby world of Cape Town underclasses, against the class ideology of Coloured social aspirations, and in the fraught world of prison itself, is vividly depicted.

Serote's *To Every Birth its Blood* and Sepamla's *Third Generation* both pay tribute to the generation of schoolchildren and adolescents who shifted township consciousness to a more purposeful mode, and took on the idea of violent revolution and the possible sacrifice of their lives. On the 16th of June 1976 20, 000 Soweto school children marched in protest against the enforcement of an earlier rule that Afrikaans had to be one of the official languages of school instruction. 176 lives were lost in a week, and more than 160 communities around the country became involved in protest. Soweto 1976 crystallized many long simmering grievances against the Bantu Education policy of 1953, which was education for subservience and basic labour; influx control, and the police presence in African life. With most policemen being Afrikaans-speaking, the school language policy drew even more antipathy. The industrial colour bar, lack of housing, rising unemployment, and the lawlessness of the security police were further issues. In 1960 the decolonization emphasized in England by Macmillan's "Winds of Change" speech had in fact assisted the Nationalists to formulate a blueprint of an internal "Commonwealth" of associated states including the Bantustans; now the actual liberation of Angola and Mozambique encouraged resistance to the tyrannical controls that the state had evolved. The loss of citizenship was a related issue, and these novels reveal that not only were there many fixed urban African communities, but writers like Serote and Sepamla, who are both also poets, had given the urban African presence and certain specific townships lyrical voice and cultural cohesiveness.

The first section of Serote's *To Every Birth Its Blood* is the most sustained first-person narrative expression of modern black urban consciousness in South Africa. It draws on the idiom of blues and jazz, showing how American culture had been adapted in Transvaal townships by the sixties, and uses the metaphor of the "journey" for music, sexuality, travel, politics and life itself (Jacobs 1989). Sustained lyrical sections on music and meditations on women anchor the urban consciousness in an awareness of daily suffering in overcrowding, arrests, alcohol, family abuse, and the impact of racial politics on sexuality and family life. The shifting moods of Alexandra township come to life: the township is a "graveyard" yet "the silence here is graceful" (12). Influx laws have made the place a "terrible stew", a makeshift place created by "schizophrenics" like H.F. Verwoerd (22). The movement of the narrative is like the improvisations of jazz, searching memory, impressions of the street, shifting moods of weekday and weekend. A recording subjectivity is recognized: "Memory can be an unreliable mirror" (222). Tsi spends his money on alcohol, is having an affair outside his marriage, quarrels with his family, and has little hope for the future. His conversations with friends register an African urban dialect that is politically aware, ironic, streetwise. Yet there is a sense that Africans, too, need a second birth into political consciousness. Tsi and his friend are subjected to physical abuse under arrest; they debate homeland politics, and their own position as journalists and photographers who are partly detached from the daily struggle. Political debates become part of the substance of fiction, more fully than in La Guma's work. Connections with women, and admiration for their beauty and individuality, create a sense of solidarity across gender divides.[4]

Part II switches to third person narrative and multiple centres, with Oupa as a young activist, and Tsi as an occasional recording presence. The deaths of young activists create a sense of historical crisis and urgency, and Alexandra as a battle site. In response to this, young people play a more active role, and are changed by their participation. Play extracts, poems and slogans are quoted. The neo-colonial attitudes of major forces like the United States are discussed. Forces within South Africa are "locked in a tight embrace" which will destroy them (106). The affiliation with Afro-American culture is not rejected, but South Africa is perceived as different, with specific political problems. The nation is perceived as being healed and remade in the days of Soweto '76: "a new, a brand-new black woman and man had been created" (133). Tsi's generation have become witnesses to the "terrible beauty" that is being born.[5] Metaphors of the movement intensify: "the Movement was like the Wind" (10). The realities of most women's lives, their solitude and separation from husbands and families, are recognized. When a rural area, Walmanstadt, is described, with its people living a subsistence peasant life, many forms of life are linked in the idea of "underground": the movement, miners, peasant farmers, in "hard work until the sweaty flesh shone like a star" (176). The Movement is validated in metaphorical association, recollection, defiance in country and city, the shifting across borders to Botswana, Tanzania, Zimbabwe. Serote orchestrates the construction of a new consciousness and new purpose in the family relationship of uncle and nephew, yet Oupa (Grandfather) also implies that the struggle is ancient, as ancient as the bloody birth-rite with which the novel ends.

Sepamla's *Third Generation* is a more conscious tribute to the courage of women in political defiance.[6] Sis Vi is a nurse, and her profession links her with the body and with service. As Lifa's mother she shows the links between motherhood and citizenship, or at least the political entities fighting for a new citizenship. Her torture under interrogation becomes more of an outrage because of her profession, but also a motive that eventually propels her son, Lifa, across the border for training. He attends the political trial dressed as a young woman, a crossdressing scene which emphasizes the way in which he learns from women during the course of events . Sharpeville and Soweto '76 are linked in the novel by Lifa's father, Buda B, who spent time on Robben Island as part of the PAC pass protest in 1960, and has come home determined to be apolitical. Lifa becomes the listener to his father's story, his disillusionment across the border in exiled groups and politics, but has to make his own decision. The novel depicts the strong links between South African politics and cultural groups, poetry, theatre, *Staffrider* magazine, and shows how even young urban Africans had to negotiate a difficult path between political awareness, danger to their lives and the difficult choice of exile for education or military training. 1976 is registered as a massive new point of change for African communities, but there are "no farewells or trumpets" when Lifa crosses the border after making his decision (163).

Mbulelo Mzamane, whose *Children of Soweto* depicts a world similar to Sepamla's, writes of his book as one in which "the community as a whole is the hero" (Sole 1988: 65) and as a "record of the attempt to create a new collective consciousness, for which Black Consciousness in South Africa stands" (Sole 1976: 65). Kelwyn Sole writes of the creation in these novels of "a backdrop of urban dwellers who are identified as belonging to a diverse yet communal world existing simultaneously in time to the actual events of each novel, but with a reality outside it and familiar to many black readers" (Sole 1988; 71). There is a double activation at work: "...a political community of black people is being naturalized and called into action by both the activists in the novels and by the novels themselves" (Sole 1988, 80). These novels, while describing and activating changes in urban reading patterns, also reveal a desire "to develop new ways of public behaviour and morality and new forms of character identification associated with the formation of a combative black secular conscience" (Sole 1988, 82).[7]

Serote and Sepamla's novels adapt the conventions of the novel, documentary devices, shifts in narrative point of view, the jazz idiom taken over from the fifties and an indigenized American musical tradition to the depiction of "the Power days". The two sections of Serote's novel depict ways of narrating shifts from individual awareness to socialist realism, and the difficult, dispersed geographic conditions under which such a novel was written. Nick Visser discusses the structural fluidity of *To Every Birth Its Blood* as matched by its ideological fluidity, with both having "as their source the irruption of history into the fictional project" (Visser 428). In this respect Serote's novel has parallels with the post-independence fiction of West African Writers like Achebe and Armah, where political coups form temporal incursions and a continuing backdrop of violence and illegitimacy. A poetics of blood and birth, and the non-verbal idiom of musical traditions, help to carry the vision of a changed order for the future, in which body would not be "bruised to pleasure soul."[8] The sense of many generations shapes a memory of historical sacrifice as well as the continuance in the children of the future. Such novels helped to shape a wider, socially aware reading public within the country while documenting the process of politicization. A political culture is rooted in an everyday township life while showing the relationship of "ghetto to industrial giant, labour to capital" (Sole 1988: 71). The Black Consciousness displayed is not an archaic reconstruction of a traditional past, but is shown to grow out of daily deprivations and political oppression. These novels look towards the day of freedom, the postcolonial moment, and create metaphors of its inevitability.

Chapter Nine
Nationalism, Postcolonialism, and the Politics of Representation: Lauretta Ngcobo's *And They Didn't Die*

"How was it that laws were so clear cut, when the lives they governed were so muddled....?" – Ngcobo, *And They Didn't Die*

"The hand that rocks the cradle should also rock the boat." – South African Women's slogan.

I. Representation and the Politics of Postcolonialism

Debates about the relationship of culture, ideology and the politics of literary representation are now extremely complex. Some critics have postulated that postcolonialism has to do with the "vibrant and powerful mixture of imperial language and local experience' (Ashcroft et al., 1995: 1). Postcolonialism is sometimes defined as "a continuing process of resistance and reconstruction" (Ashcroft et al., 1995: 2). Donna Palmateer Pennee has characterized a critical shift in terminology in relation to Canadian literary criticism: "the term 'representation' in literary studies has less to do with mimesis, with representing an accurate reflection of Canada (or wherever), and more to do with the question of representing the different constituencies or voices that populate the country and its literature" (Heble et al., 203). In modern democracies, as Charles Taylor has pointed out, there is now a "politics of universalism, emphasizing the dignity of all citizens, and the content of this politics has been the equalization of rights and entitlements" (Taylor 105). This politics of universalism and equal rights comes into conflict with the other major change Taylor identifies, the development of modern notions of identity, which gives rise to a politics of difference, and a cherishing of difference against the pressures of assimilation for indigenous or immigrant groups (105). The most recent victory won in the battle for the principle of equal citizenship, argues Taylor, was won by the Civil Rights movement of the 1960s. I would argue that the most recent victory in this struggle was achieved in South Africa in 1994, in the first democratic election there, a victory which also signalled a major last victory against colonialism compounded by racism. This does not mean that the literature which was produced in such a recent liberation struggle can be read as 'transparent' as Stephen Slemon has pointed out in relation to the significant theoretical work of Gayatri Spivak, Homi Bhabha, Abdul Janmohamed and Benita Parry (Slemon 235). It does mean, though, that South Africa can be usefully seen as an extreme and durable model of a colonial state where racist labour policies and migrancy laws interlocked in an economically powerful and extremely oppressive political system. In South African literature, I would suggest, it suited the white minority to collapse the nation into the white-controlled state, and it is this mystifying strategy which gives the white liberal novel in South Africa its characteristic nostalgic imprimatur. This is one of the reasons why Slemon's case is worth pursuing, that 'white' Australian, New Zealander, Southern African and Canadian literatures should be maintained within the ambit of postcolonial critique (236).

In raising these comparative postcolonial questions, ideas of the nation-state, and political questions concerning the specific historical contexts for understanding how identifications of nation and state have aided and abetted the prolongation of forms of colonial power, I am responding to the challenge offered by Ajay Heble when he writes that we need to recognize "the value of using theories and methodologies from elsewhere to rethink the national" (Heble 79). As he suggests, postmodern forms of enquiry have denaturalized "our understanding of knowledge, truth, history and power" (78). This means necessary interventions in everyday as well as literary life and critique, including institutional and community politics. Heble argues for cultural listening and counterpoint as helpful democratizing strategies. Australian novelist Paul Carter follows this line in his 'noise' project in Lecce, Italy, where he constructed a radio broadcast, *Tuned Noises*, to illustrate that speech responds contrapuntally to the random noises of the environment (Paul, interview with Carter, 1997).

Carter argues that migrancy has become a synonym for post-colonial consciousness, whereas in fact, in reserving the idea of conceptual mobility to itself it "preserves a colonialist temperament" (9). He suggests that "dialogical processes are never divorced from the historical subject's engagement with the land s/he occupies" (2). Somewhere between determinacy and randomness, texts and readers, postcolonial critics seek to engage new readings.

Reading between international relations and postcolonial theory, Phillip Darby asks: "what course is to be negotiated between the pressures for international standardization and the claims of cultural distinctiveness?" (136). In Canada a taxonomy of indigenous identities is sometimes the crux of claims to cultural distinctiveness. Terry Goldie's work has suggested that "the indigene as cultural item is similarly a result of hegemonic textualization" and is "most assuredly not-self, politically, economically, ideologically" (216, 222). This negative definition, falling within Margaret Atwood's overarching paradigm of Canadian survivors and victims, is sharply at odds with novelist Thomas King's rejection of the term "postcolonial" for Native literature in North America. King finds the terminology of postcolonial theory distressing for its implications: the starting-point for discussion is seen as the advent of Europeans in North America; there is a suggestion of progress; the struggle between guardian and ward is the catalyst for contemporary Native writing, and Native writers are cut off from their own traditions and agency, making their literature a construct of oppression, as in Goldie's definition (King 242-243). King offers the terms "tribal, interfusional, polemical, and associational to describe the range of Native writing", terms he prefers because "they identify points on a continuum for Native literature" which do not depend on the advent of colonialism for their meaning (243).

King may be throwing the postcolonial baby out with the bathwater, however, and while his terms may be accurate to Native North American literature, the term "tribal", for instance, has an unfortunate resonance for African literature and culture, where the results of colonialism are often Eurocentrically attributed to a tribal backsliding or to tribal factions. The whole project of Basil Davidson's work on the African nation-state, *The Black Man's Burden*, relies on linking the crisis of the nation-state not to tribalism but to the crisis of imported institutions within which Africans have been forced to survive after decolonization. States were built on alien European models and had little legitimacy for the African majority, who turned to "clientelism" (12) and a dependency on networks (tribal, familial, personal) which sowed chaos after independence. There may be a parallel situation in Canada for Native peoples, the result of segregation in reserves, which, though it may have consolidated some traditional cultural systems, has prevented effective participation in the public sphere. The mixture of local politics, unemployment, family distress, and the reification of Native peoples by global tourism, a portrait found in Thomas King's own fiction and which he subverts through parody and other forms of contestation, answers to this political description.

In the concept of democratic multiculturalism put forward by John Rex, there are two domains, the shared political culture of the public domain, involving citizenship, and a private, familial and communal domain (Rex 1996: 33-36). The interrelationship between these spheres is crucial to self-definition and forms of cultural survival. If we accepted his definitions of multicultural ideals and realities, built largely on migrant groups in Britain, wider acceptance might be gained for the idea of equal education for minority groups as well as privileged majorities (in countries like Britain and Canada, for instance). Rex also points out that multi-culturalism means nothing if it is not anti-racism (1996: 28).

II. African Migrations and Industrialization

Frantz Fanon wrote in *Toward the African Revolution* that the process of industrialization camouflaged racism: "the perfecting of the means of production inevitably brings about the camouflage of the techniques by which man is exploited, hence of the forms of racism " (Fanon 1967: 35). These essays evoke the spirit of the 1958 Accra Conference on African strategy and unity as historical unravelling of the 1884 Berlin conference, which carved up continents in the name and spirit of European imperialism. Fanon goes on to say that "The advent of peoples, unknown only yesterday, onto the stage of history, their determination to participate in the building of a civilization that has its place in the world of today give to the contemporary period a decisive importance in the world process of humanization" (Fanon

1967: 146). A black South African writer, Lauretta Ngcobo, echoes this thought when she says: "there is another victory to be won, if South Africa is to be restored to her space in Africa. The cultural battle. There is no other place in the continent which is less African than South Africa" (Ngcobo 1994: 570).

The humanist discourse which emerges in relation to the decolonization of Africa now co-exists with a deconstructive discourse which problematizes cultural identity, critiques the development and enlightenment paradigms for Africa, and insists on contradiction and difference in the cultural articulation of African and Afro-American identities.[1] Henry Louis Gates argues that the heritage of each black text in a Western language is "a double heritage, two-toned" and that writers of African descent "occupy spaces in at least two traditions: a European or American literary tradition, and one of the several related but distinct black traditions" (Gates 1984: 4). While "the very act of writing has been a political act for the black author (Gates 1984: 5), the structure of the black text has been repressed and treated as if it were transparent (Gates 1984: 6). Black people have always been "masters of the figurative"; saying one thing and meaning another has been "basic to black survival in oppressive Western cultures" (Gates 1984: 6).

Critics working within African and Afro-American feminism have also wanted to stress repetition and revision in black women's texts. Barbara Johnson, writing on Zora Neale Hurston, argues that Hurston's protagonist needs to "assume and articulate the incompatible forces involved in her own division. The sign of authentic voice is thus not self-identity but self-difference" (Johnson 212). Houston Baker situates narration within "a world that is itself constituted by a repertoire of stories" (Baker 224). Susan Willis, writing on Toni Morrison, says that "sexuality converges with history and functions as a register for the experience of change, i.e. historical transition" (Willis 263). Morrison, like Ngcobo, "develops the social and psychological aspects that characterize the lived experience of historical transition" and its consequences, "the alienation produced by the transition to wage labour" (Willis 265). Domestic service constitutes only a marginal incorporation as wage labour, and in Morrison's fiction "individual genealogy evokes the history of black migration and the chain of economic expropriation from hinterland to village, and village to metropolis" (Willis 265). Individual differences between women function to test the social dynamic within the group and society at large (Willis 279). Jane Bryce, discussing African Women's writing in a "post-Negritude, post-colonial reading of culture" suggests that recent writing is marked by a "self-conscious disjunction" (619) between tradition and modernity. African women writers' use of English and of the novel genre "may be seen as an implicit assertion of distance from the nostalgia for origins, a recognition of the need for a revisioning of culture and their relationship to it from a postcolonial perspective" (620-621).

When Lauretta Ngcobo contextualizes her own literary production, she also points to multiple, often conflicting allegiances. Born in 1931 in rural Natal, she was forced to flee South Africa in 1963 after persecution by the South African government and police harassment[2]. Her husband was in the first executive of the Pan-Africanist Congress, a radical group that broke away from the African National Congress in 1959 and organized the pass resistance that led to the Sharpeville massacre in 1960. He was sent to jail along with people like Sobukwe (leader of the PAC) and Mandela. Ngcobo's husband was involved in the lengthy Treason Trials which began in 1956. He was then in prison between 1960 and 1963, and a militant activist until 1969, when the couple eventually settled in England with their three children, and where Lauretta began her first novel, *Cross of Gold* (1981), a novel in which she found it difficult to keep her female protagonist alive as a focal centre (Hunter 1993: 102). Sindisiwe dies because at the time "death and destruction" were all-pervasive; "such has been the history of our struggle in South Africa" (1993: 107). At the time of writing her first novel Ngcobo found it difficult to see African women as capable of effecting change: "In South Africa... a black woman is oppressed by law, which has calcified around the old traditional customs. Under the Natal Code, for instance, a woman is a perpetual minor who cannot perform at law even when her husband is dead. She's equally incapacitated socially, economically, all round" (Bush 7). Ngcobo has also expressed ambivalence about feminism and the freedom that Western Women aspire to, while being agents of racial oppression themselves, whether in South Africa or England: "

I am not referring to the structure of institutionalized power, but to the yoke of daily injustice, to the bitterness of everyday living" (Vivan 111). She calls attention to a range of levels of oppression and draws a comparison between oppression by African men and white women: "through our man we feel the weight of the system, as well as that of law and tradition. An analogous thing happens to us in respect of the white woman: it is through her that a variety of oppressions befall us" (Vivan 112). Yet she acknowledges that white women have won rights which will benefit African women after democratization. This has been the case in South Africa, where women represented in Parliament now constitute thirty three and a third percent of the total, moving from 130th in the world to tenth place (Davis 587).

In attempting to define her place in relation to Western and African traditions, Ngcobo admits that; "Our women are caught up in a hybrid world of the old and the new; the African and the alien locked in the struggle to integrate contradictions into a meaningful new whole" (Ngcobo 1985: 82). African women had been cardboard figures in a written tradition that created contradictory images of idolized mothers and the realities of wifehood.[3] The oral tradition, though she cites a moving instance of its performance by her grandfather at her own birth, also "extolled the virtues of humility, silent endurance and self-effacing patterns of behaviour for our girls" (1985: 81). During her growing years and education she was made to feel marginalized in the educational system (35 women to 500 men when she attended university) (1985: 85). At school and university she observed the cultural clash between rural and city ways and people: "I began to feel a disfigurement of outlook, a mutilation within" (1985: 85). This may account for the strong presence she gives to rural women, and their powers of resistance, in her later novel, *And They Didn't Die*, in which the title signals defiance and survival.

In her autobiographical writing, essays and interviews, Ngcobo relates the fragmentation of cultural traditions to political processes, especially industrialization and migrant labour. The introduction of scripted literature divided society into an educated elite and an uneducated mass, and became a source of alienation. The system of migrant labour "altered beyond recognition the structures of our societies" and affected women who had traditionally played a prominent role in the transmission of oral literature (1985: 84). Urbanization in the gendered form of migrant labour for men "created... hardened divisions between men and women" (85).

The story of *And They Didn't Die*, which relates the different but politically inflected trials of an African couple, Jezile and Siyalo, sundered by multiple factors deriving from poverty, migrant labour, political activism and prison, customary law and gendered oppression, becomes the vehicle for conveying this process of "hardened division" between the sexes. The stories of their different trajectories into city life, patterns of disillusionment, economic struggle and politicization, become representative stories illuminating the complex intersections of capitalism, race and gender in South African life and their effects on rural people.[4]

Ngcobo's self-positioning in relation to literary traditions is also complex, acknowledging hybridity and multiple affiliations. She acknowledges her special feeling for Thomas Hardy's fiction, and this may have affected her creation of dignified rural people who are crushed by political and economic conditions as if by fate, and the passing away of rural communities (Vivan 106). She has also mentioned the attraction of the novel form: "The only form that I get on well with is the novel, but I want to capture the feel of South Africa at this particular time of transition" (Daymond 85). However, she feels that her emphasis on one central character and action is derived from an African tradition: "Our folklore which always pivots around the story of an individual, an important person of our tradition. The importance of the plot is created around one single character.... Each character has a certain gamut of options, which are drawn from an objective reality, even if it is then partly invented in the story" (Vivan 109).

Thematically African novels are restricted, because topics like land or factory ownership have no relevance, so the themes of European fiction become "arid, senseless, useless material" (Vivan 110). "The black writer is forced to limit himself to a few themes which deal with a society scarred by poverty and restrictions" (Vivan 110). But there is a broader theme of historical suffering: "the fundamental themes which are for us of common interest, and ask for an answer to the feelings of our people " (Vivan 110).

In her introduction to Miriam Tlali's Footprints in the Ouag (1989), Ngcobo traces the movement in black South African writing from a literature of cultural assimilation to protest. As literature tried to deal with industrialization and migratory labour, writers were bewildered: "These writers were faced with the paradox of creating or fashioning a new indigenous character, while the dynamics of the situation pointed to the destruction of the culture in which that character had to be rooted and flourish" (xi). The consolidation of white power with the Union of the provinces in 1910 " marks the Africans' first awareness of themselves as an oppressed people" (xii). A new spirit emerged dramatically in the 1970s and within that mood Miriam Tlali "writes from the heart of those turbulent cities" (xv), expressing "the wounds sustained in the collapse of our societies" (xvii), especially through women's eyes. As a result, Tlali tends to see tradition as a salvation for African people, whereas Ngcobo is much more critical of African custom. With regard to political purpose, Ngcobo says that her writing is "a social/political comment": "I believe books by the oppressed people can, ever so subtly, restore the desire for freedom and the will to achieve this" in the face of the psychological introjection of colonial images of inferiority (Bush 8).[5]

III. The Politicization of Rural Women

In *And They Didn't Die* Ngcobo's purpose was to show "how country women cope and resist the pressures of the law, how the laws of the country disadvantage them" (Bush 6). Rural women, the traditional food producers, have been without tilling and land tenure rights. Yet women have often rallied around injustice: they fought against the imposition of passes in the late 1950s; against the problem of dipping their dying cattle (dipping tanks were introduced to control disease), and the government's policy of building beerhalls for men, while not providing facilities for childcare (Bush 8). Multiple grievances led to defiance by women erupting in different regions of Natal in 1959. About 1000 women were arrested. These events, the context for the first section of the novel, record the emergence of "a vast new political constituency. No understanding of the radicalization of black politics in those years would be complete without a knowledge of the emergence and behaviour of this constituency" (Lodge 150).[6] Jezile's husband is in Durban while she struggles with her mother-in-law's persecution for her infertility. Siyalo is politicized in Durban by the evidence of social injustice, overcrowding and exploitation of labour, and is soon endorsed out as a troublemaker. During Jezile's visit she experiences the humiliations of her husband's hostel life, but is also given a glimpse of the activism of urban women who storm the beerhalls in protest. She feels a bond with city women: "how similar their situations were" (30).

Historical activities by the ANC Women's League are represented in a woman doctor and leader, Nosizwe, who illuminates aspects of political leadership during the build-up of popular resistance. The problems of traditional lifestyles are illustrated by Jezile's friend Zenzile, who dies in childbirth. We see the contradictions of Jezile's life and her growing awareness of her husband's involvement in an African patriarchal system. The difficulties of parenting are shown when both parents are imprisoned for periods of time. The contradictions of government policy, destroying rural communities while trying to preserve them artificially, are shown in intimate detail, as are impossible economic conditions in the countryside.

In the second phase of Jezile's life she is incorporated into urban domestic service while her husband is in prison. The transition from a fairly stable though distant family life to a single-mother household suggests the contradictions of human sexuality and family life in rural and urban South Africa. Jezile is accused by her mother-in-law (the custodian of customary law) of infidelity when she returns pregnant from a brief prison sentence. After Siyalo's prison sentence she is drawn into a single women's culture which supports her. She takes on domestic service in a white household and is then raped by her employer, who sends her home with the child to protect himself from arrest. Once back in the village she is disowned by her in-laws for having mothered a 'white' child. After Siyalo's release from prison he claims his daughters but he and Jezile are separated by customary law. The compounded force of racial oppression and customary law is vividly illustrated in these ironic plot twists.

In the last, compressed section of the narrative Jezile and her children move through the turbulent political clashes of the 1976 countrywide insurgency and the emergency period of the mid-eighties. Jezile's daughter Ndondo becomes a political activist and flees the country. Her son Lungi, the child of mixed race, becomes a leader at his Coloured school and is paralysed from the waist down in a police shooting incident. When her daughter Ndondo visits her secretly during the emergency period, a soldier storms their house and attempts to rape Jezile's other daughter, S'naye. Jezile kills the soldier. Jezile now goes to her husband with an account of her own rape by her employer and they realize that at the moment of a possible reunion they will be sundered by another prison sentence. The final scene is complex in its evocation of an historical abyss, the abyss of the combined historical damage of industrialization, the apartheid system, and racialized sexual abuse: "He swung around to face her, carnage in his mind, and looked at her wordlessly, penetrating those eyes, mind to mind, heart to heart. Together they drifted back in reverse into a vortex beyond recovery, in a kind of falling away" (245).

This ending also counters any emancipatory or enlightenment narrative, constituting a critique of the liberal ideology which sees modernization as inevitably progressive.[7] Ngcobo's narration during the transitional period in South Africa thus involves a memory of the complexity of historical damage to individuals, the family and the collectivity of the oppressed. Her novel is an implicit answer to the question Said poses as central to a decolonizing imagination: " How does a culture seeking to become independent of imperialism imagine its own past?" (Said 1993: 214). Published at the time of the political transition to democracy in South Africa, Ngcobo's novel answers this question by pointing to the legacy of historical damage experienced by one African family in South Africa over the decades of urbanization and resistance.

While the narrative moves toward a violent crisis and sense of historical loss, the seizing of subjectivity by those who have traditionally been seen as objects and a "subordinate race despised by all" (Wicomb 18) manifests "the material reality of people's lives" in a way which Wicomb calls moving beyond "the legacy of victims" (Wicomb 15). Ngcobo's novel demonstrates a complex relationship between social structures and subjectivity, particularly in Jezile's fully rendered consciousness as she struggles with the changing political and cultural contexts that surround her, with what Belinda Bozzoli calls "the changing material world" as " a decision-making existential being" (1991: 236).

The novel as genre is well suited to displaying the tension between internal and external struggles, conflicts between generations and genders. *And They Didn't Die* is thus anti-essentialist in effect, recognizing, like Foucault, "the manifold structures of power" with their varied forms and multiplicity of "localized resistances and counter-offensives" (Escobar 381) and thus also recognizing that "women, far from being powerless, are agents in their own fates" (Udayagiri 161). In Jezile's successful defence of her daughter's body the materiality of women's oppression is recognized and partly resolved. Female sexuality mediates systems of power, but the generational progression from Jezile to S'naye shows that self-defence is the lesson of female experience. In defending her daughter Jezile defends herself in an action that testifies to the consciousness raising she has undergone in both racial and gender politics.

IV. Pan-African Vision and Insurgent Subjectivities

Ngcobo has argued that in South Africa women's quarrel is primarily with the state, and that this differentiates their feminist struggle from many others (Bush 8). Because of her characters' involvement in radical political action her fiction could be said to be part of the discourse of the Pan-Africanist Congress. Graham Pechey characterizes two counter-texts to the Freedom Charter of 1955 and its broad universalizing humanism: the Pan-Africanist Congress and Black Consciousness (28). The PAC critique of 1959, he argues (the point in time where Ngcobo's second novel begins) "is founded in an anti-modernist narrative that reduces everything to a story of repossession" (28). *And They Didn't Die* could be said to participate in this anti-modernist discourse and in the radical politics of the PAC, but it feminizes this discourse and offers a critique of liberal discourse and earlier women's writing in South Africa by revisioning key tropes. Instead of the seduced and abandoned white settler women who characterize the novels of Olive Schreiner and Pauline Smith, and whose stories are played out in terms of white settler hegemony and patriarchal social codes for settler women, Ngcobo's protagonist Jezile is politicized by multiple forms of gender and racial oppression to the point of militancy and an act of violence. Seduction is replaced by rape, indicating the structural and personal violence the state inflicts on African women, and their economic and personal vulnerability in domestic labour.[8]

The liberal use of the adoptive situation in Schreiner's novel *From Man to Man* (1926), where a white woman adopts the child of her husband's liaison with a Coloured servant, is also revised when Jezile bears a Coloured child from her employer's rape and the child becomes an activist in radical clashes with the state and the military. This situation allegorizes the national situation: European interbreeding with an indigenous and slave population produced the people whose partial alliance with Black Consciousness helped to oust them from power. Ngcobo's reworking of this narrative trope inverts Sarah Gertrude Millin's notorious use of mixed blood as the sign of laxity and degeneration (Coetzee 1988). The revised adoptive family evokes the spirit of non-racial resistance that marked the eighties in South Africa and the rise of associations such as the United Democratic Front.

This image of a mixed-race family born out of colonial violence participates in a current ideological discussion around nation-building in South Africa, and what Willem van Vuuren has called "the specific problem of 'rainbow-nation' multiculturalism" versus the "African hegemony of African nationalists" (Bristol conference paper, 1999: 1). More specifically, "Coloured." identity as a category has been problematized within the politics of meaning and deconstruction by Thiven Reddy, who suggests that "all labelling categories are equally unstable and in South Africa, the stability of the non-Coloured categories is a function of the word and sign 'Coloured'" (Bristol conference paper, 1999: 2). This deconstructive approach contrasts with the materialist analysis of Adam Habib and Sanusha Naidu, who draw on electoral data for the run-up to the 1999 elections to illustrate the "electoral heterogeneity within these communities" (Coloured and Indian). They conclude that the reluctance of lower income Coloured and Indian voters to vote for the African National Congress is the "result of the simultaneous application of an affirmative action policy with a neo-liberal economic program, the results of which enhance the material vulnerability of the poorest sectors of the Indian and Coloured communities" in South Africa (Habib and Naidu, Bristol Conference paper, 1999). Ngcobo's mixed-race family metaphor is an inspirational one which perhaps mystifies these material divisions within actual political constituencies, but it speaks the historical atmosphere during the resistance period of the eighties.

And They Didn't Die evokes the existential dimension of the cultural dislocations, land expropriations and economic disempowerment imposed by colonialism, industrialization and migrant labour. By appropriating narrative, one of the forms of cultural control, and subverting it to oppositional purposes, South African writers circulate new histories, in this case making rural women's consciousness in previously "hidden struggles" available to new readerships (Beinart and Bundy). The intersections of customary law, African patriarchy and apartheid legislation are revealed in the detailed emotional texture of family life.[9] The destructive personal effects of migrant labour are graphically presented: sexual loneliness, enforced adultery, arrest for those politicized in the cities, the degradation of the physical and social environment, "a hopeless patchwork of effort, determination, and failure" (Ngcobo 221; Ramphele 1991). The slow collapse of subsistence agriculture is the context of the opening chapters, and the women's grievances are related to the extension of influx control legislation in the Bantustan (homeland) policy designed to prevent permanent African settlement and thus political franchise in the cities (Walker 1982).

At the same time the novel provides a fictional record of the construction of patterns of resistance and solidarity, the ways in which currents of freedom rippled through rural communities and in moments of private reflection and understanding:

> ...she knew she had taken a decision that she should have taken ages before. Nobody would ever take that power away from her – not his mother, not her own mother, not anyone. Both mothers had had such a hold on her precisely because they had never had that power over their own lives –" (11).

The lifting of women's local resistance to new levels is shown in the prison experience of the village women:

> Then suddenly, somewhere in the deepest part of that jail, they heard a different kind of song. It pierced the prison air and shattered the

> silence of the vast corridors. The women in the cells listened for a few moments. Then they knew it was Nosizwe. They picked up her song and sang it with gusto. Her song was not a hymn, it was a political song that throbbed in the gut. Their voices returned to them full of strength and defiance. They grew strong and threw off the feeling of inadequacy that had gripped them. (100-101).

The links between the fifties decade, which Ngcobo describes as the beginning of "political confrontation with the oppressor" (Intro. to Tlali 1989: xii) and thus of a new type of literature, and the township uprisings of the seventies and eighties are telescoped in the last section of the novel, in the story of Jezile's children (Mzamane 1985). Ngcobo's position within the generation of writers produced by Sharpeville and its political contexts is unique, as Mzamane has pointed out, because she carries to an English-speaking audience the rural experiences and subjectivities usually produced in indigenous languages or in the liberal patriarchal, morally recuperative format of Alan Paton's *Cry, the Beloved Country* (Mzamane 40). The English language and the multi-generational realistic family saga are adapted to become the vehicles of a South African narrative of dispossession and resistance. Ngcobo adopts the documentary devices of incorporating political speeches, lists of grievances, historical dates and protests, devices that have been central to historical fiction and its use by South African novelists such as Nadine Gordimer (Clingman 187-8). Rural families living on the reserves are made into what Raymond Williams calls a "knowable community", shaped by a novelist "in such a way as to give it identity, presence, ways of reusable articulation" (Williams, 165-182). *And They Didn't Die* is the only substantial prose narrative to detail the subjectivities of rural South Africans, especially women, as they responded to all of the major historical crises in South Africa.

Ngcobo's insistence on a cumulative plot movement toward an act of violent retaliation against sexual violence suggests the role played by gender awareness in black South African women's writing, and its relationship to state violence and the aftermath of colonialism (Head, Mvula, Qakisa, Tlali 1984). The conclusion of the novel, while evoking solidarity between Jezile and Siyalo, also draws the limits of the body as metaphor. The body, writes Jean Comaroff, is "a tangible frame of selfhood," which "mediates all action upon the world and simultaneously constitutes both the self and the universe of social and natural relations of which it is a part" (Comaroff 6-7). The South African legacy is still immured in forms of violent control and aggression inflicted on women (Hansson). J. M. Coetzee's novel, *Disgrace*, extends the South African debate on gendered and state violence by narrating a double story of transgression in the post-apartheid era: an incident of sexual harassment on a college campus, and a violent attack and the rape of a white woman (the professor's lesbian daughter) by young Africans at an isolated farmhouse. His novel opens up the debate on gendered and racial violence over the post-apartheid boundary, and questions the different forms of gendered violence or appropriation of women in relation to state formations and decolonization. The "vortex" that concludes Ngcobo's novel, by contrast, in a moment of turbulent silence, is an index to the historical semi-occlusion of rural African predicaments in the mass migrations to cities, under apartheid, and in the emergence of an educated, urban African elite.

The story Ngcobo tells is also the story of African women's labour: "the country women are the backbone of the South African superstructure" (Bush 8). They maintain homes for absent husbands, supplement meagre wages, produce and raise the next generation of workers (Bush 8). The labour of serfs generally, as J. M. Coetzee has pointed out, was elided in the late nineteenth century South African pastoral. The rural labour of African women has been doubly elided in white South African fiction, except for occasional glimpses, such as the one we get in Gordimer's *July's People*, which is in a displaced futuristic setting. Ngcobo makes visible what Njabulo Ndebele calls "the unacknowledged presence of Black labour and the legitimacy of the political claims based upon that labour" (1994: 4). The differentiated process of labour incorporation for men and women, and the different costs, are detailed within a family setting which is repeatedly shattered by punitive state interventions.

Ndebele has pointed out that the role of literature in the crisis of transition is not an easy one: "It throws up a problematic of its own within the broad cultural crisis" (9). Ngcobo's novel, written within that crisis, looks backward and forward, finding an avenue "in the history of the survival culture of the people" (8). Though *And They Didn't*

Die, as Eva Hunter has argued, works within a broad framework of historical and social referentiality (Hunter 1994: 120), subjectivity is shown as constructed within what Benita Parry calls "antagonistic forces and heterogeneous signifying practices, solicited and situated by conflicting ideological addresses" (Parry 22). These ideological addresses include radical PAC politics, racialized gender violence, anti-apartheid activism, and a critique of customary African law. Ngcobo's novel is a form of anti-pastoral that looks backward over sixty years to Sol Plaatje's Barolong couple, Mhudi and Ra-Thaga, embedded in visionary pastoral romance in his novel, Mhudi. In that novel a married couple in the nineteenth century wars of African conflict became the vehicle of colonial critique and a prophetic vision of further dispossession in the colonial encounter. Ngcobo's novel looks back toward that moment, records its consequences, and registers forms of survival beyond colonialism.

The insistent narrative focus on Jezile and her shifting subjectivity " affirm cultural identity as a new and insurgent subjectivity that has been fought for and reconstructed in the process of struggle" (Parry 22). The story Ngcobo tells in *And They Didn't Die* is the story of what cannot afford to be forgotten in the construction of a democratic future for South Africa. Ngcobo is in accord with Fanon's pan-African vision when she writes of the relationship between South Africa and the rest of Africa: "Where the white government sees state barriers, we see gates, not to enter and pillage or encroach on other people's territories but to enter in good will, and together with fellow Africans we shall create a new impregnable African continent." (Ngcobo 1991: 199). This gendered metaphor, willing an African renaissance into being, records the ways in which the story of colonial violence has always been a story of gendered violence. At the same time it suggests a new basis for communities in Africa, including South Africa, one of good will and co-operation beyond the violent legacy of colonialism. Whether or not this more benevolent future becomes a reality involves what Anne McClintock calls "rethinking the global situation as a multiplicity of powers and histories that cannot be marshalled obediently under the flag of a single theoretical term" and engaging in a politics of affiliation (McClintock 396).

Chapter Ten
"Postmodernism of the Homeless": Racial and Sexual Politics in Nadine Gordimer's *None to Accompany Me*

"My country is the world, whole, a synthesis. I am no longer a colonial.
I may now speak of my people." – Nadine Gordimer, *Writing and Being*

Postcolonialism and postmodernism are now highly contested terms, their valencies partly determined by the cultural locations within which they are defined. If one accepts Gayatri Spivak's dictum that "there is no such thing as postcolonialism" (Attwell 104), then any attempt to find historical equivalencies, historical postcolonial junctures such as political or constitutional independence, or actual postcolonies, is rendered meaningless. "Postcolonialism" becomes a critical hypothesis, like "postmodernism". Yet the former term, even if it is understood as only another way of reading, a focus for interpretation, carries a burden of political meaning and historical scrutiny, whereas the latter is attached to an aesthetic or philosophical periodization of culture. In Canada the triumphal march of fiction from provincialism to postmodernism described by Linda Hutcheon has been questioned for its homogenizing tendencies, for precluding "the study of what is historically specific to our postcolonial experience and our present cultural condition" (McDonald 43).[1] Diana Brydon has argued for the continued usefulness of a postcolonial reading strategy as a "locally situated, provisional, and strategic attempt to think through the consequences of colonialism and to imagine non-repressive alternatives to its discursive regime" (10). Complex formulations of the duplicity of reading and writing, of the tension between performative and pedagogical in language and culture, have been offered in the work of Homi Bhabha, and have spread from diasporic intellectuals to those contesting the power of liberal humanist critique and racially organized political oppression in countries like South Africa.[2] At certain periods of political emergency in South Africa, as in the mid-eighties, one South African critic rejected postmodernism as a bland international conspiracy "conducted in the coteries of art" (521) and was led to the paradoxical conclusion that certain plays by Athol Fugard and Nadine Gordimer's novel *A Sport of Nature* should not have been written at all. Imaginative literature of a certain kind, inadequate to political suffering, should be silenced (Chapman). In this way self-styled radicals became new censors. Michael Chapman's critique of *A Sport of Nature* rested on the sexist view that the protagonist, "screwing her way up the African high command" (525) should have been still-born. Women, unlike men, use sex to gain power.

In the context of African Studies, the formulations of postcolonialism and postmodernism have been no less various.[3] The "postcolony", argues Achille Mbembe, is a plurality of spheres and arenas, in which postcolonial subjects must continually improvise (Werbner 1). Werbner and Ranger's *Postcolonial Identities in Africa* opens postcolonial studies to a major field of social analysis: "the cultural politics of identities in transition within postcolonial Africa" (2). As African societies emerge from a history of colonial violence, "the postcolonial imagination… reconfigures personal knowledge in everyday life" (3). Imaginative literature is one of the chief means to such reconfiguration, and in South Africa some critics have argued persuasively that it is in the effective imaginative ordering of ordinary life that a dimension of convincing and dignified interiority is to be gained, after decades of protest rhetoric (Ndebele). Werbner seeks an accommodation between "the postcolonial as postponement" and the damaging colonial legacy in Africa (4). Earlier scholarly emphasis on the underdevelopment of Africa has led to a view of victimhood that has often obscured agency, the power of resistance that eventually produced political decolonization. One question then becomes whether or not postmodernism, with its emphasis on irony, decentering and self-reflexivity, has not also obscured the cultural presence and popular resistance of colonized subjects. Robert Thornton has stressed postmodern elements in the South African transition of the nineties. The explosion of old political certainties and identities, he argues, has led to the subversion of all signifiers, though this might seem to fly in the face of continued reports of violence, the continuing legacy of apartheid, and endemic economic inequality (145). Thornton understands 'apartheid' (the historical regime) as mainly a bureaucratic administration, "one of the most virulent varieties of modernism" (141). If one accepts this definition of pathology, then the breaking open of boundaries, the acceptance of multiple identities, provisional selves, decentering, play and reflexivity, become strategies that contest the earlier totalizing power of colonial and apartheid narratives of identity. This seems particularly important in South Africa, where essentialized ethnic identities became the grounds of long maintained political oppression (Ranger 274).

Nadine Gordimer's 1994 novel, *None to Accompany Me*, seems to be designed to test the limits of postmodernism.[4] Endlessly preoccupied with the socio-political flux of the nineties, with the now apparently permeable borders between Europe and Africa, and with the provisional politics of the pre-constitutional period, the novel nevertheless points to certain boundaries, forms of damage and immobility which are the legacy of the apartheid era. One of these is the right to shelter and housing:

> Now on the horizon, a vast unloading of scrap without any recognizable profile of human habitations, now at the roadside, the jagged tin and tattered plastic sheets that are the architecture of the late twentieth century as marble was the material of the Renaissance glass and steel that of Mies Van der Rohe; the squatter camps, the real Post-Modernism: of the homeless. (81)

Gordimer's late fiction, usually demarcated from the publication of *The Conservationist* (Newman, King), has increasingly recognized that life in any culture is a process toward knowledge of an indissoluble but finally unknowable self. This paradoxical process, the slippage between self and world, continuity and change, past and present, is enacted at many levels in *None to Accompany Me*. It is part of the narrative construction of memory and desire in Vera Stark's consciousness, a woman divorced after World War II and ending her second marriage in the present context of political transition to democracy in South Africa. Indeterminacy is also imaged in the novel's use of photography to stress the role of perception, the questionable relationship between motive and identity, loyalty and betrayal in political and personal life (Ettin). Twice in the novel, by a mother and then a son, photographs are used to record the presence of a new lover and convey a subliminal message to others. The "signature" that scrolls before Vera Stark finally on her breath in the night air is a marker of identity, but also tenuous (324). The structural headings of the novel: "Baggage", "Transit" and "Arrivals" point to mobility and process.

None to Accompany Me can thus be read as a postmodern extension of the way in which Gordimer's fiction has been preoccupied with the relationship of narrative to power, and Africa to Europe. It represents anew, and differently from her earlier *July's People*, the crucial time of political transition, now not imaged as apocalypse and crisis, but as a further phase of established relationships and processes, embedded in everyday life, part of the *longue duree* needed in "periodizing the postcolonial" (Werbner 5). The handling of time and chronology in the novel underscores the necessity, in South Africa, of "permanent transition" (Thornton 158), perhaps another name for democracy. The unfolding of events in past and present illustrates that "the recesses of the domestic space become sites for history's most obsessive invasions" (Bhabha 9) in the portrayal of change and decay within two families, one white South African family, the Starks, and one black South African family, the Maqomas, recently returned from exile. The distortions of family life caused by political pressures such as exile, cultural dislocation, the shock of return after years of absence, and the negotiation of new political identities, affect the Maqomas. The inversion of gender roles in their marriage, with the wife, Sibongile, becoming increasingly successful and active in political life, takes a toll on their marriage and intimacy. The involvement of an ex-Robben Island prisoner, Oupa, in their daughter's life, leads to an abortion. This abortion, and the death of Oupa after a car hijacking on the road, seem to endorse and yet question Vera Stark's insight that the personal life is transitory, while political life and art are transcendent (305). The close relationship between political and personal life seems to belie Vera's perception. The critical distance between narrative voice and Vera as persona stages the complex nexus of individual perception in process. So does the flux of political life itself, the marvellous rendering, in narration and dialogue, of the key issues of political reconstruction. We witness the legacy of apartheid working itself through into new forms of crime and poverty, and squatter camp leaders like Zeph Rapulana emerge as corporate figures of power. Zeph Rapulana is a figure of African dignity and quiet integrity, and his role as peasant intellectual draws a connection between the rural areas and urban centres of power, the previously polarized sites where Gordimer has located her interrogation of the geography of apartheid, the homeland system, and the asymmetrical effects of apartheid laws.

Gordimer herself once defined her subject as the historical inadequacy of liberalism in South Africa (1961: 51). This inadequacy has been imaged in a series of cross-racial encounters, most powerfully in cross-racial relationships between white women and black South African men (Knox). These relationships have gradually deconstructed both white colonial fear and ignorance, which she imaged as a "dark house" where writer and reader wander about in "extraordinary and terrifying intimacy" (1961: 38), and the stereotype of the black South African as the vessel of sensuality and desire.[5]

In *None to Accompany Me* the Starks have had a marriage based on happy sensuality and heterosexual companionship, but it fades because they respond unequally to the challenges of their time and place. The husband, Ben, places all his stock in personal love, and the wife eventually finds his dependency and obsession a burden. The novel records the growth in Vera Stark of "a new capability", a social and human connectedness created through work in a nonracial organization, the "Foundation" (122). This new connectedness is eventually imaged in her tenancy at Zeph Rapulana's house, an inversion of housing patterns which is a microcosm of the new political dispensation. At the end of the novel she collides with a young African woman in a 'dark house', a woman with "the sap-scent of semen" on her (323). This scene represents both a psychological incorporation of African 'female other' and a letting go of sexual rivalry with younger women, yet it does imply, as Karen Lazar has argued, that older women are desexualized under the sign of patriarchy (115). The motives for the decay of the Stark marriage are not clearly portrayed, except as the atrophy of sexual need itself, and a weariness with the absolute value the husband has given to personal love. The space occupied by the "Foundation", which investigates the effects of social engineering and forced removals, mediates private and political concerns and becomes a symbol of the reconstruction of state power. It also serves as the basis of the new civil space which critics like Schulze-Engler have argued is needed in South African post-apartheid society (Clayton ARIEL 1996). The friendships Vera Stark develops with Oupa and Zeph Rapulana have their basis in this shared zone of work towards a common social goal.

The narrative methods Gordimer employs in *None to Accompany Me* exemplify the crisis of representation implied in postmodernism. As Fanon has pointed out, "the time of liberation is... a time of cultural uncertainty and, most crucially, of significatory or representational undecidability" (quoted by Bhabha, 35). The narrative works within what Homi Bhabha has called a "Third Space", as "unrepresentable as the self," which constitutes the discursive conditions of enunciation that ensure that the meaning and symbols of culture have no primordial unity or fixity; that even the same signs can be appropriated, translated, rehistoricized and read anew" (37). The novel is much concerned with the reappropriation, the circulating difference, of gestures, features, rooms, houses, objects, people and relationships. One significant instance occurs in the changing uses of a Johannesburg flat, 121 Delville Wood, a few decades earlier the clandestine retreat of Vera Stark and her lover "Hitler baby" Otto Abarbanel (69). The flat is reappropriated by a second generation of (black) South African lovers, Oupa Sezake and Mpho, a young beautiful black girl born and educated in European exile. The apartment block's name is in itself a colonial appropriation of the Great War, the one before the "definitive war" (4). World War II seemed to have a final resolution, VE Day, unlike those political revolutionary struggles whose culminating phase is being sketched in this particular novel, in all of its cultural complexity and complicity, with old alliances constantly breaking up into new configurations, "without the resolution of victory parades" (4).

This reads like a postmodern citation of the triumphalist ending of *A Sport of Nature*, but it works as a powerful reminder of the role of the military in enforcing racial oppression and creating situations of civil war in South Africa. "Delville Wood." has now become an apartment block habitable by black South Africans moving into the inner city area, in a reversal of the earlier forced removals from city slums to rural 'homelands', yet overcrowding remains. An intertextual reference to Alan Paton's *Cry, the Beloved Country*, the marker of an even earlier wave of African urbanization of rural men, is found in the term "umfundisi" (reverend) which Vera uses teasingly to her comrade in hiding, Didymus Maqoma, who once visited her disguised as a clergyman. This process of reappropriation occurs in hand gestures with Otto and Raphulana, in the passing on of house spaces, and in the genetic memory of faces as the narrative notes Ben's features resculpted in his daughter Annick. As the story of the "Hitler Baby" indicates, genetic inheritance is also open to manipulation.

One of the central images of the novel, suggesting both mimesis and postmodern play, is the sculpted torso, an image with which Part II closes. The torso was created by Ben for Vera, "exceptionally explicit of the power of the body" and yet, in the passing on of the sculptures to the lesbian couple, "transformed into the expression of desire between woman and woman" (228). The torsos operate as ambiguous symbols of sexual identity, of a process of repeated loss and recuperation of self, and endless disguises of self. The body is registered as inescapably present, the particular flesh of individuality and desire, as a younger Vera has been in a transforming, betraying moment in 121 Delville Wood by a lover, Otto, himself transformed from Jewish victim into an Aryan product of Hitler's genetic engineering. This scene, like the sculpted torsos, is an ambiguous comment on the nature of desire and the perverse workings of power, questioning feminist definitions of female sexuality. Victim/victimizer is a split sign at this physically unifying moment in the novel, like the power reversals of politics, and sexuality itself is seen as having strange triggers within multi-layered male and female identities. Some historically layered complexities blaze together in sexual moments; others have to be sifted through in the endless process of the political renegotiation of power and land which moves South Africa towards its first democratic election in 1994. The novel is dense with an awareness of the damaging political past of a country which "got it all wrong" (261). No-one's life is untouched by the weight of that past as they struggle for understanding and reform in the present.

The body also has its own integrity and limits, which we see defined in the physical humiliations and distortions undergone by

Oupa Sejake as he dies in an Intensive Care ward after he and Vera are attacked on an isolated country road. The incident, a much later reworking of Gordimer's early story "Is There Nowhere Else We Can Meet", shows how black South Africans are now also targets of robbery, as they have crossed from oppression to some forms of power and affluence. The scene, as in La Guma's fiction, makes a link between common crime and politics, one introduced in Oupa's stories of Robben Island prison, and hinting at other colonial and postcolonial forms of theft. The bullet which pierces Vera's leg in the same incident nevertheless links her to Oupa for a while in life and even more decisively with his family of mourners in the grief which follows his death. The death of Oupa (Grandpa, a title of respect which ousts the colonial pejorative 'boy', aligning youth and age differently, respectfully) is contrasted with the death of the white grandfather, happening routinely within Vera's home. Home and outside, the supposed public sphere, are continuously exchanged, compared, reinscribed one within the other. Bodies like the young Mpho's exist at complex intersections of African and Western codes which give her beauty new meaning. Her body can also be impregnated by Oupa, producing a fetus which is aborted and yet replaced, with gender-switching, in the 'black' infant, a girl, adopted by the lesbian couple. Consequences continuously and unsettlingly unfold out of other consequences, shifting individuals and relationships into new formations.

Though Gordimer is known for her relegation of feminist struggle to a very secondary role in relation to the anti-apartheid struggle, the postmodern opportunity offered in narrating post-apartheid as a liberation for Vera Stark is also an opportunity to critique patriarchal codes. Dorothy Driver has argued that literary criticism in South Africa has often turned on the gendered assumptions of the culture/nature binary, with masculine and feminine social constructs endorsing racial constructs. What is needed is the unsettling of "phallic definitions of culture and nature", and their unmasking as social constructs (460). *None to Accompany Me*, the first Gordimer novel to show a woman moving definitively beyond sexuality and marriage, unsettles many of these binaries. In the Stark marriage, as mentioned, it is the wife who assumes her right to involvement in the public world, who takes sexuality outside marriage as her right, who sees her grandchildren more coolly than her husband, and who eventually jettisons the house originally given to her by her first father-in-law, with all its implications. Vera's unconventional coupling with her ex-husband after rejecting him for a new lover, and her adulterous affair with Otto during her second marriage, argue for women's sexual freedom, even during marriage, with the spontaneity of her responses and insistence on pleasure as a form of what Irigaray calls "disruptive excess" (Grosz, 191). The Maqoma marriage offers similar subversions of conventional gender roles. More significant subversions of cultural authority happen at the level of event and plot, making nonsense of the conventional culture/nature binary. The main device here is the double paternity of Ivan, Vera's son and image.

Vera does not know whose child her son Ivan is, having coupled with her visiting first husband at almost the same time that her lover, Bennett, is moving in as her second husband. This rather radical form of undecidability in private life destabilizes any notion of generational succession or patrilineal inheritance, the underpinnings of the racialized gender hierarchy, colonialism and land ownership (Coetzee). At the end of the novel we still don't know whose son Ivan is; neither does Vera. Since the son Ivan is cast exactly in Vera's image, she can never know whose son he is. This paternal undecidability is her secret, though at times it seems almost to be an open secret, in Alice Munro's implied sense of the intimate knowledge which passes from ourselves to others without ever being publically formulated, and which we become more adept at as we age. To Zeph Rapulana, Vera speaks of Adam, Ivan's son, as "my son's young son" which he corrects to "grandson". To that "grandson" who can never be fully known as a grandson, she almost confesses the "secret" which he senses around his father's birth. Knowledge does not seem to be the point; rather, Ivan becomes a figure who problematizes the usual boundary between nature and culture, the incest taboo, and the kinship system which has been the racialized basis of land ownership and property inheritance. Perhaps unconsciously, Vera's actions have cuckolded both her husbands, each being used to cuckold the other, with biological succession and thus cultural power rendered very murky and unstable. The undecidable paternity challenges traditional maternity with something closer to parthenogenesis: Vera, we are told "reproduced herself, only herself, in male form, for her new lover" (275). This process short-circuits the exchange of Vera from husband to husband, subverting the female object status this might have implied. It also undermines the certainty of paternity traditionally desirable in loyal and stable marriages, the basis of patriarchal law, heterosexist behaviours, and a racial order, literalizing a feminist challenge to patrilineal authority and traditional succession (Homans).[6]

A second literalization is found in the passing on of household bedrooms: Ivan, the son's bedroom, which it pleases Ben to give to Adam, his grandson, as a "destined occupancy" for a line of male children, is accepted by Vera because she perceives that it has in the meanwhile been occupied by her daughter and her lesbian partner, and thus "imposed no succession upon a male. So here he could be himself, whatever that might turn out to be" (249). Adam can be the first man and reinvent a more tolerant humanity after this breaking of the patrilineal order. The lifting of binary gender oppositions and patrilineality thus frees both female and male heirs. As Elizabeth Grosz argues in defence of Luce Irigaray's theory: "the body's morphology is the effect of the intervention of dominant discourses and their creation of human subjects as their reflections" (Grosz 189). Irigaray posits two major elements of female corporeality usually disavowed in the history of Western thought: "the question of maternity and the question of female sexuality" (189). In *None to Accompany Me* the protagonist is not only sexually autonomous and excessive; her repeated double-dealing in sexual desire has made her son's paternity uncertain and possibly influenced her daughter towards lesbianism. The evolving discussion of lesbianism in the novel is one way in which the novel reconstructs reader responses along with Vera's.[7]

Vera broaches the subject first with friends and then more openly with Annick herself. Annick and Lou become adoptive lesbian parents of a 'Coloured' child, an event symbolizing another way of reconstructing family and nation. Vera's almost comic insistence on the wonders of the penis and the physical attributes of her lover-husband becomes laced with irony when she outgrows the need for her stud altogether. As in *My Son's Story*, it is the wife who becomes politically active in unexpected ways, and the husband who ends up in unwanted solitude. Vera's celibacy at the end of the novel, however, forecloses some of the questions of sexual politics and feminism. Her apparent rejection of her husband's body has to be poised against Oupa's country wife's enforced acceptance of her husband's dead body. A contrast between forms of constraint and choice has been one of the chief means Gordimer has employed in all her fiction to demonstrate the gross inequities created by a system of legalized racial domination.

Vera's lifelong insistence on her sexual autonomy and pleasure opens out into a new dimension which has always been latently there, a capacity for impersonal care and a bonding with men exclusive of desire. The relationship Vera develops with Zeph Rapulana, crucially mediated by her witnessing her protege, Oupa's death after the attack on a country road, becomes an image of this new relationship, one arising from, and helping to bring into being, a new social order without need for control, intrusion or domination. This new cross-cultural relationship which is more than friendship, because it is built on the sacrifice and mortality which is both accountable to and beyond political history, becomes an image of the ideal sexual relationship: "to accept one another for exactly what they were.... this was the basis that ought to have existed between a man and a woman in general" (282). It is surely significant that Vera's relationship with her new landlord, living in an "annexe" which reverses colonial annexation, develops as her marriage fails. Bourgeois marriage in South Africa is revealed retrospectively as a chrysalis for a new self, but also a husk that contained the apartheid order. As in *July's People*, bourgeois marriage is shown as coterminous with a racial order; the departure from one is a departure from both.

The textual space of undecidability, of constantly shifting cultural signifiers, in an era when "what would seem the most impersonal matters are the most intimate" (296), thus becomes a space within which "the abandonment of an old personal life" is made possible (315). Vera, selling off her dishonestly acquired house, symbolic of the old South African order, moves into a new relationship with herself, dancing alone in "an exaltation of solitude" (306). This solitude, which is still socially meaningful, has been guaranteed by a continuing investment in the people and the places she lives among, not handing them over to any entirely private, oblivious commitment to married love, as her husband has done. Yet now the "brotherhood" of the political revolution is also revealed as ambiguous and fractured; when the vagrant who attacks Vera and Oupa puts his arm through the window he calls Oupa "brother". Similarly, the heroic image of the African National Congress is troubled by revelations of interrogation camps and Didymus Maqoma loses political credibility for his role in such a camp. Here, too, the absolute binary of oppressor and oppressed is problematized. The moment of heroic narrative has passed.

Though *None to Accompany Me* invokes certain moments in which a handclasp between man and woman is a seal on their belonging together "as a single sex" (123) without desire, and such moments celebrate what Oupa calls "the real meaning of brother" (15), of social love, Gordimer's fiction never lets go of what Vera calls "my own point of view, you know, because I'm a woman" (177). In writing of the process of recent political change in South Africa, Gordimer unfolds the lineaments of a sex which is and is not one, writing not "about or for women, but, rather, as a woman" (Grosz 194).

None to Accompany Me shows that postmodernism can serve the interests of postcolonial vision, of a radically decolonized consciousness. It also serves to depict a cultural system based on shifting alliances rather than essentialized identities, at a time when all of the old certainties based on a South African segregationist system have been called into question. The self-reflexivity of the novel does not undermine the depiction of gender, class and racial constraints, but shows them as multiple, shifting determinants of behaviour over different generations. The novel now serves a vision of South Africa which is criss-crossed by many identities, departures and returns, across internal dissolving borders of cities and rural homelands, and between South Africa and Europe.[8] New forms of freedom, sexual self-expression, personal mobility and family structures seem to be available. Against this Gordimer sets an abortion for Mpho and Oupa's child, and an intense focus on Oupa's mortality. These images, in their invocation of the death of an ex-Robben Island prisoner in a new form of violence which is yet an old form of poverty in Africa, register the losses and sacrifices over many generations that have to be set against new freedoms. The finitude of death is contrasted with the apparent indeterminacy of postmodernism.

Notes

Chapter One
1.　In his critique of the "writing-back" paradigm as a norm in Ashcroft, Griffiths and Tiffin's *The Empire Writes Back*, Frank Schulze-Engler argues that this model locates the dynamic of historical and cultural agency in a hypostasized 'centre'; local contexts are devalorized; it also cripples the potential of theory because it cannot deal with other political conflicts that lie outside the politics of decolonization (31-32).

Chapter Two
1.　Michael Wade's study of the South African novel is sub-titled "Inscriptions of Skin-Colour" and it makes racial classification, guilt, and exclusions central conceptual terms. Abdul JanMohamed argues that "...the colonial mentality is dominated by a Manichean allegory of white and black, good and evil, salvation and damnation, civilization and savagery, superiority and inferiority, intelligence and emotion, self and other, subject and object". This binary structure is repeated in his comparative groupings of three white and three black authors. He simplifies colonial psychology into "rejection and dependency on the part of the colonizer, and attraction and hatred on the part of the colonized." My readings are not meant to underestimate the damaging effects of the state legislation, censorship and ghettoization which Mphahlele, among many others, has emphasized (*The African Image* 1962: 109).

2.　Christie, MacLennan and Hutchings consider only two black writers in the fourteen novelists they discuss. They write very dismissively of Plaatje's *Mhudi*, and tend to subsume criticism into a liberal humanist project.

3.　　In their note on "hybridity" in *Key Concepts in Post-Colonial Studies* (1998), Ashcroft, Griffiths and Tiffin point out that "hybridization takes many forms: linguistic, cultural, political, racial, etc" (118). Bakhtin used it to refer to multi-vocal narratives; Homi Bhabha to stress the mutual construction of subjectivities between colonizer and colonized. Robert Young has pointed out the dangers of a term used in the imperialist context to connote regression and biology or genetics. I have used the term in an attempt to break out of the binary model of criticism in South Africa which tended to replicate apartheid structures, and to suggest that the whole context in which the English South African novel appeared was already culturally syncretic. I have attempted to trace cross-racial influences and borrowings or forms of intertextuality, while respecting the political construction of racial boundaries, spaces and differences, in particular by referring to specific politically enacted laws and prohibitions in South Africa.

4.　　Other forms of cross-cultural affiliations and traditions have been suggested: D. J. Opperman pointed out that the White South African poetic tradition passed from Pringle through Leipoldt to Campbell, and on to Van Wyk Louw (Gray 31). Mbulelo Mzamane has traced the continuation of an oral tradition in later black South African poets and novelists such as Oswald Mtshali, Mongane Serote, and himself (Mzamane 1984). Liz Gunner has suggested that the praise poem has been a continuing vehicle of cultural production (Gunner 1995). Mike Chapman has pointed out the shared and cross-racial features in South African literature: an allegorizing, morally purposive tradition which links Olive Schreiner, Alan Paton and Nelson Mandela (Chapman 1996: 51) . M. J. Daymond has suggested that black women writers like Kuzwayo and Ngcobo are occupying a space partly cleared for them by white women writers such as Schreiner (Daymond 1996, Introduction). In some cases the writers themselves have endorsed this, such as Bessie Head and Ngcobo (Head 1989, 17; Ngcobo in Vivan 1989). In the theoretical formulations of women's autobiography in South Africa, cross-cultural linkages have emphasized a valorizing of a communally identified self (Coullie 1996). Albie Sachs has argued that broad, flexible definitions of South African culture are not only historical but necessary for the forging of a postapartheid society that values a varied creativity (Sachs 1990).

5.   Isabella Matsikidze asks of Bessie Head's fiction: "How does the fiction address its subjects' multidimensional political identities in relation to nationalist goals and to the cyclical evolution of the nation." She relates the experience of some of Head's protagonists to the nationalist condition of their textual worlds (140), and to gender struggles, suggesting diverse causes of gender conflicts.

6.   Cherryl Walker points out key differences between Western and African constructions of motherhood. "Western middle-class conventions of mothering are underpinned by silence, passivity, and women's confinement to the domestic realm" (423). This ideology is at work in *The Story of an African Farm*. In South Africa physical care of children has often been delegated, to a nanny, to township caregivers, or extended family, and the "intersection of motherhood and waged employment" (426) is differently textualized by white and black South African women, for obvious reasons. Tlali gives some attention to the conflict between 'mothering', whether of one's own or other people's children, and various political pressures within the workplace or township life. Walker also points out the enduring value of fertility for African women, the uncoupling of African marriage and motherhood in the twentieth century, and the importance of Christianity in the construction of African motherhood in the modern period.

7.   Scottish missionary John Ross arrived at a mission station in the Eastern Cape with a Ruthven printing press in 1823. This led to the encouragement of black writing both in the vernaculars and English at Lovedale Institution, at Morija Press in what is now called Lesotho, and Mariannhill in Natal (Visser 1976). Visser points out a distinction between R. R. R. Dhlomo's *An African Tragedy* and Plaatje's *Mhudi*, that the former was written for a mission press, Plaatje's published by one" (45). R. H. W. Shepherd wrote in 1945: "...the greatest call on African (literary) powers will probably come through the medium of the novel" (*Lovedale and Literature for the Bantu: A Brief History and a Forecast*, Lovedale: Lovedale Press, 1945). Quoted by Visser, 49.

8.   Kelwyn Sole has suggested that in the depictions of African communities in post-1976 novels Tlali is unusual in that "the extended family in *Amandla* (1980) seems to be the link mediating the individual characters' relationships to the larger community" (Sole 1976: 72).

9. Gwen Bergner writes: "In addition to a sex-gender economy that organizes men into social groups through the distribution of women, there is an economy regulating the distribution of women so as to construct and perpetuate racial groupings. In the colonial context, the operative "law" determining the circulation of women among white men and black men is the miscegenation taboo, which ordains that white men have access to black women but that black men be denied access to white women. Both incest and miscegenation taboos enforce culturally dictated categories of permitted and prohibited sexual relations. But the race-sex economy of colonialism also produces a hierarchical relation between the groups of men it delineates " (81). Horst Zander has pointed out some of the probems in depicting inter-racial love when the society classifies it as sick. The reader is either made an accomplice of the society which taboos miscegenation (as in Lessing's *The Grass is Singing*) or trapped inside a particular psychology (as with Magda in Coetzee's *In The Heart of the Country*), (Zander, 95, 107).

Chapter Three

1. Dorothy Driver offers a complex discussion of the tension between motherhood and writing for South African women writers, especially in relation to Black Consciousness, in her "M'a-Ngoana O Tsoare Thipa ka Bohalleng – The Child's Mother Grabs the Sharp End of the Knife: Women as Mothers, Women as Writers." *Rendering Things Visible*. Ed Martin Trump : 225-255. Driver argued (in 1990) that "South Africans are called upon to define themselves in terms of the oppositions offered by the symbolic repertoire of apartheid, a repertoire which includes the marks of imperialism and colonialism, of class exploitation, racial oppression, and gender stereotyped expectations" (232).

2. The society depicted on Schreiner's farm belongs to what Giliomee characterizes as a "settled frontier society living on what can be called the closing frontier... From the Afrikaner point of view, settlement embraced notions of occupation of the land and control over all its resources; colonization involved not only the conquest of land but also the incorporation of the indigenous peoples; while lack of power usually had two dimensions – ineffective control by the white government over its own frontier offshoot (periphery) and the inability of any of the communities to establish its hegemony in the frontier zone. For

Aficans, as Martin Legassick has pointed out, the frontier meant something quite different: it was the first stage of a process in which their political power was eroded as they were absorbed into plural communities, and in which their material and social bases were transformed through their integration into a market economy linked with the industrializing and capitalist economy of Europe" (see Giliomee 78; Legassick's PhD dissertation "The Griqua, The South-Tswana and The Missionaries, 1780-1840. The Politics of a Frontier Zone" and his chapter in *The Shaping of South African Society*: 243-90.)

3.   Tant Sannie's resistance to new farming methods towards the end of the novel, and the whole direction of life on the farm towards an expurgation of liberal elements as forms of authority are consolidated, are fictional representations of what Gilliomee characterizes as a broad, non-specific process of sociopolitical consolidation," a series of closings based on different aspects of the frontier. These comprise (1) economic closure, manifested in growing land and scarcity of resources, a shift from subsistence to commercial farming, and increased control of the means of production by a specific class; (2) growing social stratification as discrete "races" or ethnic groups merged into a plural society with a given set of caste or class relationships; and (3) political closure, in the imposition of a single source of authority " (79).

4.   David Cowart proposes four categories of historical representation in fiction: 1) The Way It Was: authors aspire to historical verisimilitude; 2) The Way it Will Be: authors reverse history to contemplate the future; 3) Turning Point: authors seek to pinpoint the precise historical moment when the modern age or one of its features came into existence; 4) The Distant Mirror: authors project the present into the past (Cowart 4). *The Beadle* participates in mode 4, whereas Schreiner uses mode 3 in *African Farm* in scenes such as the invention of a sheep shearing machine to pinpoint the moment of industrial modernity, and mode 2 in the futuristic allegory in *From Man to Man*. In Mode 1, entering the mental life of the past, which Smith does with the Little Karoo inhabitants, can be a way of challenging cultural superiority and offering a more credible version of specific cultural realities. Smith does this with regard to English cultural superiority, as "township" writers would later portray urban black life to challenge white cultural ignorance.

5. "Lacan sees, in a way similar to Levi-Strauss, the Oedipus complex as the pivot of humanization, as a transition from the natural register of life to a cultural register of group exchange and therefore of laws, language and organization" (Sarup 8).

6. Ampie Coetzee writes: "At the time of the invention of a tradition of Afrikaner nationalism, and the conscious creation of a literature in Afrikaans at the beginning of the century, the importance of a national consciousness was recognized in the production of literature" (323).

7. Smith's novel, usually claimed as a cameo of English liberal fiction, represents a post-war foundational phase of the process of ethnic and cultural mobilization by Afrikaners, which Ampie Coetzee has divided into two early phases: 1875-1922 and 1922-1948 (324). During the first phase there were literary sketches on the evils of the city, a concern for the demise of feudalism and the poverty of white share-croppers, nostalgia about the waning of the farm idyll and the promise of a new, bourgeois future for whites (329). The final moment of the text, one in which a young 'poor white' Afrikaner woman is incorporated into family succession and the social order without marriage, reveals both a rejection of English influence in South Africa, which had until then controlled the state and dominated the economy, and the problematic situation of women vis-a-vis patriarchal culture and class. The biological succession imaged in three generations is one of Afrikaner consolidation, not entry into bourgeois culture, though Andrina's child is the herald of new national formations.

Chapter Four

1. For overviews of the literary context, see Tim Couzens, "The Social Ethos of Black Writing in South Africa: 1920-1950." *Aspects of South African Literature*. Ed. C. Heywood; Ursula Barnett, *Vision of Order: A Study of Black South African Literature in English* (1914 – 1980. Also Albert Gerard, *Contexts of African Literature, African Language Literatures,* and A. C. Jordan, *Towards an African Literature: the Emergence of Literary Form in Xhosa*. More specific works on Plaatje are listed in the Selected Bibliography. Mphahlele provides a thorough summary of the "events that conditioned and refined the culture of the African people in

the nineteenth and early twentieth centuries": "frontier wars; vehement missionary evangelism and the establishment of church schools, teacher-training institutions and presses; the upsurge of journalistic writing, the entrenchment of the white man's political supremacy, and apparent negation of the Christian faith as the new converts understood it; the conflict between Christian and traditional values at a time when the missionary had established in the mind of the convert the idea that to be Christian was to be civilized and vice versa; the dramatization of self by the newly converted Christians; the formation of Union; the Native Labour Regulation Act of 1911 and the Natives Land act of 1913; the founding of Fort Hare College in 1916 and of the South African Native Congress in 1912, following closely upon, and responding to, the end of the Boer War and the formation of Union." (1992. 43) Mofolo's *Chaka*, written in 1910 in Southern Sotho but only published in 1925, provides a vernacular example of counter-colonial mythologizing in its presentation of the Zulu emperor as a tragic figure rather than a bloodthirsty monster. R. R. R. Dhlomo's novella *An African Tragedy* (1928) predates the publication of *Mhudi* but presents city life from the rural Christian point of view as wholly evil. Mphahlele suggests that *An African Tragedy* and H.I.E Dhlomo's long poem – Valley of a Thousand Hills" (1940) "create a whole picture of the African as disoriented man, of his landscape as wasteland" (1992, 48).

2. For a comprehensive biography see Brian Willan's *Sol T. Plaatje: South African Nationalist 1876 – 1932*. London: Methuen, 1984.

3. "Mfecane" is a word of Xhosa origin meaning "the crushing" used for the coastal wars; "difaqane", which now seems to be a preferred term from Sotho, is used for the wars in south-east Africa in the early nineteenth century, and connotes forced migrations (Marks and Atmore 2). Plaatje chose for his historical terrain "points of interaction" between colonizers and indigenous peoples, but also reveals "an internal dynamic of various social formations" (Marks and Atmore 2). As in Achebe's *Things Fall Apart*, the power of the narrative comes from the vivid sketching of indigenous societal and cultural patterns and views white colonial incursion from that perspective.

4. A proliferation of independent churches followed the Land Act. One dramatic incident occurred at Bulhoek, where Enoch Njijima's Is-

raelite sect, who squatted at Bulhoek, near Queenstown, defied the government in 1921. They suffered grievous loss of life when their leader's prophecy led to their attack on police (Davenport 178).

5. T. T. Moyana offers a summary of various early censorship laws: the Entertainment (Censorship) Act of 1931; the Customs Act (1955); the Publications and Entertainment Act (1963). The Publications Control Board was established in 1963. See also Nick Visser on "Censorship and Literature" in *Perspectives on South African Literature*. He discusses the Publications Act of 1974 and the Internal Security Act 74 of 1982. J. M. Coetzee's *Giving Offence: Essays on Censorship* (Chicago: U of Chicago P, 1996) discusses South African censorship in an international context. The style and tone of *Mhudi* suggest an artistic method intended to work within the Lovedale missionary ethos while achieving artistic and political aims of its own.

Chapter Five

1. See the special issue of *Current Writing on South African Literature and Postcolonialism* edited by David Attwell, *Current Writing* 5, 2 (1993).

2. I.D. MacCrone's *Race Attitudes in South Africa* (1937) discussed the set of psychological assumptions underpinning racist attitudes in South Africa, and "unveiled the uniformity of thought in white South Africa" (J. Davis, Introduction, xxvii).

3. Denoon discusses South African English status as similar to that of "bywoners", "living on Afrikaner land, enjoying the privilege of almost equal status with the landlord, and distinguished sharply from the African labourers" (222).

4. Cornwell sees Millin as the "mature heir of a tradition " which included "Kellson's Nemesis" by W. C. Scully (1895); *Jan, an Afrikander* by Anna Howarth (1897); "The Out Span" by J. P. Fitzpatrick (1897); *Souls in Bondage* by Perceval Gibbon (1903); *Of Like Passions* by Francis Bancroft (1907); *The Heir Of Brendi ford: A South African Sketch* (1909). At the same time, he argues, an oppositional tradition of liberal response was unfolding in works like *Leaven* by Douglas Blackburn (1908); *Margaret Harding* by Perceval Gibbon (1911) and Plomer's *Turbott Wolfe* (1925).

5. Wole Soyinka argues that La Guma's *A Walk in the Night* (1964) "provides a more profound and disturbing insight into humanity than we find in the visionary piety of his fellow countryman Alan Paton or the multi-racial vision of Peter Abrahams" (*Myth, Literature and the African World* 64). Kolawole Ogungbesan sees *The Path of Thunder* as the culmination of the first phase of Abrahams's literary career and says: "On the personal level, interracial love is the real test of race relations. It is a symbol of the freedom of the mind from hatred and fear, a negation of the herd instinct as represented in the traditional societies by tribalism and, in the modern states, by apartheid" (177).

6. See Michael Alexander's biography of Paton, *Alan Paton: A Biography*. Oxford: OUP, 1994. Also Paton's autobiographies, *Towards the Mountain: An Autobiography* and *Journey Continued: An Autobiography*.

7. In 1957 the Nationalist Government "went ahead with its plans to attack integrated higher education, in the face of strong opposition from those universities (all of them English-medium) which were not already uniracial. " Objections were overridden and after widespread demonstrations the measure was carried on 11 June 1959 (Davenport 275-6).

8. See Gareth Griffiths, "The Myth of Authenticity" in *The Postcolonial Studies Reader*. Eds. Ashcroft, Griffiths and Tiffin. London: Routledge, 1995.

Chapter Six

1. Under his own government (1924-33) Hertzog, who took the Portfolio of Native Affairs, declared in 1925 that "territorial segregation of the natives is the only sound policy that can be followed for both the natives and the Europeans in South Africa." This depended on the Africans learning how to develop the reserves both agriculturally and industrially. He linked this with the idea that in the towns, on railways and in existing industrial undertakings, the white man was entitled to first consideration. Thus, as Davenport points out, the reverse side of segregation, conceived as a favour to the black man, was the industrial colour bar (Davenport 205).

2.

3. Selby Msimang was active in trade union politics and helped to establish the Industrial and Commercial Workers' Union (I.C.W.U.) which might have been the nucleus of a formidable labour movement, but there was little support from Natal or the Transvaal. The alliance between Msimang and Clements Kadalie disintegrated, and Msimang withdrew from trade union politics (Davenport 180).

4. *Cry, the Beloved Country* was an international success, and was translated in Norway, Sweden, Denmark, The Netherlands, Finland, Czechoslovakia, France, Italy, Israel, Greece, Yugoslavia, Spain and Portugal. See Edward Callan, *Alan Paton*, Boston: Twayne, 1982.

Chapter Eight

1. The statistics in the above section and throughout the chapter are from John Kane-Berman's *Soweto: Black Revolt, White Reaction*.

2. Kelwyn Sole writes: "The events of 1976 have a powerful implied presence as a fulcrum in this narrative, transforming the organized subjective narration of Tsi Molope in the first section into a more objectified focus on the activities of the group of revolutionaries afterward" (Sole 1988: 65).

3. "Martin Legassick has cogently argued that whereas the earlier policy of segregation was at bottom an attempt to apply a system of extra-economically controlled labour to mining and farming, apartheid was the application of a cheap forced labour policy to secondary industry, which came into its own after the Second World War as the main growth sector in the economy" (Davenport 374). See Martin Legassick, "Legislation, Ideology, and Economy in post-1948 South Africa," *Journal of Southern African Studies* 1, 1 (1974): 5-34.

4. Sole points out the inconsistent and often stereotypical portrayals of women in this fiction, their association with domesticity, a pornography of torture (Sepamla, *Ride the Whirlwind*, 157), and the use of a trite romanticism in Tlali's *Amandla*, despite her portrayal of women as actors in social life (Sole 1988: 79).

5. W. B. Yeats: "All is changed, changed utterly. A terrible beauty is born." ("Easter 1916")

6. Sole identifies a group of novels within a resurgence of fiction in the 1970s: Tlali's *Muriel at Metropolitan* (1975) and *Amandla* (1980), Ahmed Essop's *The Visitation* (1980) and *The Emperor* (1984), Sipho Sepamla's *The Root is One* (1979), *A Ride on the Whirlwind* (1981) and *Third Generation* (1986), Mzamane's *The Children of Soweto*, Serote's *To Every Birth Its Blood* (1981) and Boyd Makhoba's *On the Eve* (1986). I have selected a few texts more directly concerned with a process of politicization leading up to exile for the purposes of further, militarized resistance.

7. A policy of rapid distribution among black readers was developed by Ravan Press during the seventies and eighties for *Staffrider* magazine, and for their published fiction. *To Every Birth Its Blood* went into a second print run of 1,500 copies in late 1985, and by August 1986 a third print-run was considered after excellent sales (Visser 422).

8. W. B. Yeats: "Where body is not bruised to pleasure soul \ Nor blear-eyed wisdom born out of midnight oil. \\ O chestnut tree, great rooted blossomer \ Are you the leaf, the blossom or the bole? \ O body swayed to music, O brightening glance \ How can we tell the dancer from the dance?" ("Among School Children").

Chapter Nine

1. Mridula Udayagiri writes that "development has been a problematic concept, because it perpetuates unequal relations in the global economy, and ignores perceptions of progress that may be very different from those of policy-makers "(Marchand and Parpart 1995: 160). She also suggests that theories of development and underdevelopment "remain firmly anchored in emancipatory paradigms that emerged in the Age of Enlightenment" (160).

2. Biographical details are taken from the interview by Robert Bush, "Do Books Alter Lives?" *Wasafiri* 1, 1 (Autumn 1984): 5-8.

3. Zoe Wicomb says ambivalent social attitudes towards women are rather like those that characterize writing itself: "the consecration of women as virgins or mothers or other fetishizations of women which at the same time allow women as human beings to be treated with contempt" (Wicomb 1994: 574).

4. Margaret Daymond writes in her introduction to *South African Feminisms* that the essays in the collection "begin to uncover a history of complicity between apartheid ideology and the patriarchalism of nineteenth-century Calvinism, tracing an overlap between the institutionalization of racial 'apartness' and masculinist epistemology" (Introduction x-xi).

5. Carol Boyce Davies describes African feminism as " a hybrid of sorts"; there is "a struggle against women's own internalized oppression" (241). For Ngcobo this struggle clearly took place over time in her increasing confidence in representing rural women's lives in fiction.

6. Brian Worsfold gives an excellent account of the political context for the novel in his article on Ngcobo in *Altered State: Writing and South Africa*.

7. Ngcobo had been pressured by her first publisher, Longmans, to add an optimistic epilogue to *Cross of Gold* (Bush 7).

8. Jackie Cock discusses the South African domestic worker as one instance of the "trapped worker".

9. Customary law offered forms of protection but at the cost of the woman's loss of autonomy in communally identified functions within marriage and childbearing (see Nhlapo). Independence, migration, and incorporation into urban wage labour brought a new set of problems, economic insecurity, and often a neo-colonial repackaging of patriarchy (see Jochelson, also Cheater and Gaidzwana). Mahmood Mamdani's discussion of the "bifurcated state" is the most thorough analysis of the relationship of state formations to family and civil society to date (Mamdani 1996).

Chapter Ten

1. As McDonald points out, and as Hutcheon's own work makes clear, she has always insisted on "postmodernism's essentially political character" (McDonald 40).

2. Kelwyn Sole has recently published a thorough overview of the diverse critical perceptions and debates in South Africa as they have contested and refined postcolonialism and postmodernism. He suggests that "South African 'postcolonialists'... generally feel an urge to ground

their notion of discursive productions within historical contexts and ideological struggles" (123). An earlier overview by Annamarie Carusi also questioned the limits of postcolonial models in the South African context.

3.   Karin Barber has recently focused on a neglected topic, the elision of "modern indigenous language expression in colonized countries" by postcolonial studies (4).

4.   Dominic Head discusses aspects of postmodernism in *None to Accompany Me* in his review of the novel.

5.   Kathrin Wagner's book-length analysis of Gordimer's fiction canvasses the topics of psychosexual distortion and ambiguity in her representation of black South Africans.

6.   Margaret Homans's insights into nineteenth century women writers' revision of "the cultural myths of women's place in language" (5) can be usefully extended to twentieth century women writers.

7.   Judie Newman offers a summary of Gordimer's key devices in answering the question "Whose story is it?" by establishing a counterpoint between male and female protagonists, white and black interpreters; by employing double plots which readjust the relationship between social context, text and subtext; by the reconstruction of the implied reader; and by interrogating the linguistics of the South African cultural voice" (14). The language code switching in the novel is complex and registers a new flexibility in cross-cultural communication, but this is another topic.

8.   See the interviews with returned exiles in *Out of Exile: South African Writers Speak*. Interviews With Albie Sachs, Lewis Nkosi, Mbulelo Mzamane, Breyten Breytenbach, Dennis Brutus, Keorapetse Kgositsile. NELM Interview Series, No. 5. Grahamstown: National English Literary Museum, 1992

Selected Bibliography

Abrahams, Peter. *Mine Boy.* London: Heinemann, 1946.

Abrahams, Peter. *Path Of Thunder.* New York & London: Harper & Brothers, 1948.

Abrahams, Peter. *Return to Goli.* London: Faber & Faber, 1953.

Ahmad, Aijaz. *In Theory: Classes Nations, Literatures.* London: Verso 1992.

Alexander, Michael. *Alan Paton: A Biography.* Oxford: Oxford University Press, 1994.

Anderson, Benedict. *Imagined Communities: Reflections on the Origin and Spread of Nationalism.* London: Verso 1983.

Ashcroft, Bill, Gareth Griffiths and Helen Tiffin, eds. T*he Empire Writes Back: Theory and Practice in Post-Colonial Literatures.* London: Routledge, 1989.

Ashcroft, Bill, Gareth Griffiths and Helen Tiffin, eds. *The Post-Colonial Studies Reader.* London: Routledge, 1995.

Ashcroft, Bill. "Against the Tide of Time: Peter Carey's Interpolation into History. " *Writing the Nation: Self and Country in the Post-Colonial Imagination. Critical Studies* Vol 7. Ed. John C. Hawley. Amsterdam-Atlanta, GA: Rodopi, 1996. 194-213.

Ashforth, Adam. *The Politics of Official Discourse in Twentieth-Century South Africa.* Oxford: Oxford University Press, 1990.

Attwell, David. "Interview With Homi Bhahbha." *Current Writing* 5, 2 (1993): 100-113.

Baker, Houston A. Jr. "To move Without Moving: Creativity and Commerce in Ralph Ellison's Trueblood Episode." *Black Literature and Literary Theory*. Ed. Henry Louis Gates, Jr. New York: Methuen (1984): 221-248.

Barber, Karin. "African Language Literature and Postcolonial Criticism." *Research in African Literatures* 26, 4 (1995): 3-30.

Barnett, Ursula. *A Vision of Order: A Study of Black South African Literature in English (1914-1980)*. Cape Town: Maskew Miller Longman, 1983.

Barsby, Christine. "Olive Schreiner: Towards a Redefinition of Culture." *Pretexts* 1, 1 (1989): 18-39.

Bazilli, Susan. *Putting Women on the Agenda*. Johannesburg: Ravan Press, 1991.

Beeton, Ridley. *Facets Of Olive Schreiner: A Manuscript Sourcebook*. Johannesburg: Ad Donker, 1987.

Behr, Mark. *The Smell of Apples*. New York: St. Martin's, 1995.

Beinart, William. *Twentieth Century South Africa*. Oxford: Oxford University Press, 1994.

Beinart, William and Colin Bundy. *Hidden Struggles in Rural South Africa*. London: James Currey, 1987.

Bergner, Gwen. "Who is That Masked Woman? Or, The Role of Gender in Fanon's Black Skin, White Masks." *PMLA* 110, 1 (1995): 75-88.

Berkman, Joyce Avrech. *The Healing Imagination of Olive Schreiner: Beyond South African Colonialism*. Amherst: U of Massachusetts P, 1989.

Bhabha, Homi. *The Location of Culture*. London: Routledge, 1994.

Blau DuPlessis, Rachel. *Writing Beyond the Ending: Narrative Strategies of Twentieth Century Women Writers*. Bloomington: Indiana UP, 1985.

Boehmer, Elleke, Laura Chrisman and Kenneth Parker. *Altered State?: Writing and South Africa*. Mundelstrup: Dangaroo Press, 1994.

Bonner, Philip. "'Desirable or Undesirable Basotho Women': Liquor, Prostitution and the Migration of Basotho Women to the Rand,

1920-1945." *Women and Gender in Southern Africa to 1945.* Ed. Cherryl Walker. Cape Town: David Philip, 1990. 221-250.

Bozzoli, Belinda. "Marxism, Feminism and South African Studies." *Journal of Southern African Studies* 9 (1983): 139-171.

Bozzoli, Belinda, with Mmanto Nkotsoe. *Women of Phokeng: Consciousness, Life Stratedy and Migrancy in South Africa, 1900-1983.* Portsmouth: Heinemann, 1991.

Bradford, Helen. "Women, Gender and Colonialism: Rethinking the History of the British Cape Colony and Its Frontier Zone, c1806-1870." *Journal of African History* 37, 3 (1996): 351-370.

Brennan, Teresa. *History after Lacan.* London and New York: Routledge, 1993.

Breytenbach, Breyten. *Mouroir.* Farrrar, Straus, Giroux, 1985 .

Breytenbach, Breyten. *True Confessions of an Albino Terrorist.* New York: Farrar, Straus, Giroux, 1985.

Brink, Andre. *Imaginings of Sand.* London: Secker and Warburg, 1996.

Brink, Andre. *The True Life of Adamastor.* London: Secker and Warburg, 1993.

Brink, Andre. *On the Contrary: A Novel, Being the Life of a Famous Rebel, Soldier, Traveller, Explorer, Reader, Builder, Scribe, Latinist, Lover and Liar.* Boston: Little, Brown, 1993.

Broe, Mary Lynn and Angela Ingram, ed. *Women's Writing in Exile.* Chapel Hill: U of North Carolina P, 1989.

Brydon, Diana. "Introduction: Reading Postcoloniality, Reading Canada." *Essays in Canadian Writing* 56 (1995): 1-19.

Brydon, Diana and Helen Tiffin. *Decolonizing Fictions.* Sydney: Dangaroo, 1993.

Bundy, Colin. "Land and Liberation: popular rural protest and the National Liberation Movements in South Africa, 1920-1960." *The Politics of Race, Class and Nationalism in Twentieth Century South Africa.* Eds. S. Marks and S. Trapido. London: Longman, 1987. 254-285.

Bunting, Basil. "The Origins of Apartheid." *Apartheid: A Collection of Writings on South African Racism by South Africans.* Ed. Alex la Guma. New York: International Publishers, 1978.

Bush, Robert. "Do Books Alter Lives?" *Wasafiri* 1, 1 (1984): 5-8.

Carusi, Annamarie. "Post, Post and Post. Or, Where is South African Literature in All This?" *Ariel* 20, 4 (1989): 78-95.

Casaburri, Ivy Matsepe. "On the Question of Women in South Africa." *Whither South Africa?* Ed. Bernard Magubane and Ibbo Mandaza. Trenton, NJ: Africa World Press, 1988. 137-160.

Casey, Janet Gallighani. "Power, Agency, Desire: Olive Schreiner and the Pre-Modern Narrative Moment." *Narrative* 4, 2 (1996): 124141.

Chapman, Michael. "The Liberated Zone: The Possibilities of Imaginative Expression in a State of Emergency." *Perspectives on South African English Literature.* Ed. Michael Chapman, Colin Gardner, Es'kia Mphahlele. Johannesburg: Ad. Donker, 1992. 514-542.

Chapman, Michael. "Mandela, Africanism and Modernity: A Consideration of Long Walk to Freedom." *Current Writing* 7, 2 (1995): 49-54.

Chapman, Michael. *Southern African Literatures.* London: Longman, 1996.

Cheater, A. P. and R. B. Gaidzwana. "Citizenship in Neo-Patrilineal States: Gender and Mobility in Southern Africa." *Journal of Southern African Studies* 22, 2 (1996): 189-200.

Christie, Sarah, Geoff Hutchings and Don MacLennan. *Perspectives On South African Fiction.* Johannesburg: Ad. Donker, 1980.

Clayton, Cherry. "Women Writers and the Law of the Father: Race and Gender in the Fictions of Olive Schreiner, Pauline Smith, and Sarah Gertrude Millin." *English Academy Review* 7 (1990): 99-117.

Clayton, Cherry. *Olive Schreiner.* New York: Twayne, 1997.

Clayton, Cherry, ed. "Writing the New South Africa." *Ariel* 27,1 (January 1996).

Clingman, Stephen. *The Novels of Nadine Gordimer: History from the Inside*. Johannesburg: Ravan Press, 1986.

Cobbing, Julian. "The Mfecane as Alibi: Thoughts on Dithakong and Mbolompo." *Journal of African History* 29 (1988): 487-519.

Cock, Jacklyn. "Trapped Workers: Constraints and Contradictions Experienced by Black Women in Contemporary South Africa." *Women's Studies International Forum* 10, 2 (1987): 133-140.

Coetzee, Ampie. "Literature and Crisis: One Hundred Years of Afrikaans Literature and Afrikaner Nationalism. " *Rendering Things Visible*. Ed. Martin Trump. Athens: Ohio UP, 1990. 322-366.

Coetzee, J. M. *Dusklands*. Johannesburg: Ravan, 1974.

Coetzee, J. M. *In the Heart of the Country*. London: Penguin 1977.

Coetzee, J. M. *The Life & Times Of Michael K*. London: Secker & Warburg, 1983.

Coetzee, J. M. *White Writing: On the Culture of Letters in South Africa*. Johannesburg: Radix (in association with Yale UP), 1988.

Coetzee, J. M. *Age Of Iron*. London: Secker and Warburg, 1990.

Coetzee, J. M. *The Master of Petersburg*. London: Secker and Warburg, 1994.

Coetzee, J. M. *Giving Offence: Essays On Censorship*. Chicago: University of Chicago Press, 1996.

Coetzee, J. M. *Boyhood: Scenes from Provincial Life*. London: Secker and Warburg: 1997.

Coetzee, J. M. *Disgrace*. London: Secker and Warburg, 1999.

Comaroff, Jean. *Body of Power, Spirit of Resistance*. Chicago: U of Chicago P, 1985.

Comaroff, John. L. T*he Boer War Diary of Sol T. Plaatje: An African at Mafeking*. Johannesburg: Macmillan, 1973.

Cornwell, Gareth. "The Early South African Novel of Race." *Perspectives on South African Literature*. Eds. Michael Chapman, Colin Gardner, Es'kia Mphahlele. Johannesburg: Ad. Donker, 1992. 75-93.

Coullie, Judith Lutge. "(In)Continent Islands: Blurring the Boundaries between Self and Other in South African Women's Autobiographies." *Ariel* 27, 1 (1996): 133-148.

Couzens, Tim. "The Dark Side of the World: Sol Plaatje's *Mhudi*." *English Studies in Africa* 14, 2 (1971): 187-203.

Couzens, Tim. "Sol Plaatje's *Mhudi*." *Journal Of Commonwealth Studies* 8, 1 (1973): 1-19.

Couzens, Tim. "The Social Ethos of Black Writing in South Africa 1920-1950." *Aspects of South African Literature*. Ed. C. Heywood. London: Heinemann, 1976. 66-81.

Couzens, Tim. Introduction to *Mhudi*. London: Heinemann Educational, 1978.

Couzens, Tim. "Widening Horizons of African Literature: 18701900." *Literature and Society in South Africa*. Ed. Landeg White and Tim Couzens. Pinelands, Cape: Maskew Miller Longman, 1984. 60-80.

Couzens, Tim."Sol T. Plaatje and the First South African Epic." *English in Africa* 14, 1 (1987).

Couzens, Tim and Stephen Gray. "Printers and Other Devils: The Texts Of Sol Plaatje's *Mhudi*." *Research in African Literatures* 9, 2 (1978): 198-215.

Cowart, David. *History and the Contemporary Novel*. Carbondale: Southern Illinois UP, 1989.

Crail, Archie. *The Bonus Deal*. Regina, Canada: Coteau Books, 1992.

Crais, Clifton. *The Making of the Colonial Order: White Supremacy and Black Resistance in the Eastern Cape: 1770-1865*. Cambridge, England and New York: CUP, 1992.

Cronwright-Schreiner, S.C. Introduction to *From Man to Man (or Perhaps Only...)*. London: Unwin, 1926. Republished with an introduction by Paul Foot. London: Virago, 1985.

Crush, Jonathan, Alan Jeeves and David Yudelman. *South Africa's Labour Empire: A History of Black Migrancy to the Gold Mines*. Boulder: Westview Press, 1991.

Darby, Phillip. *The Fiction of Imperialism: Reading Between International Relations and Post-Colonialism.* Lonon: Cassell, 1998.

Davenport, T. R. H. *South Africa: A Modern History.* 2nd edition. Johannesburg: Macmillan, 1978.

Davidson, Basil, Joe Slovo, Anthony R. Wilkinson. *Southern Africa: The New Politics of Revolution.* Harmondsworth: Penguin, 1976.

Davis, Jane. *South Africa, A Botched Civilization: Racial Conflict and Identity in Selected South African Novels.* Lanham UP of America, 1997.

Daymond, M. J. "Some Thoughts on South Africa, 1992: Interview With Lauretta Ngcobo." *Current Writing* 4, 1 (1992): 85-97.

Daymond, M. J. *South African Feminisms: Writing, Theory and Criticism, 1990-1994.* New York and London: Garland, 1996.

Denoon, Dennis. With Balam Nyeko and the advice of J. B. Webster. *South Africa Since 1800.* London: Longman, 1972.

Derrida, Jacques. "Racism's Last Word." *'Race' Writing and Difference.* Chicago: U of Chicago P, 1986.

Dhlomo, R. R. R. *An African Tragedy.* Johannesburg: Lovedale Press, 1928.

Driver, Dorothy. *Pauline Smith.* Johannesburg: McGraw-Hill, 1983.

Driver, Dorothy. "M'a-Ngoana O Tsoare Thipa ka Bohaleng–The Child's Mother Grabs the Sharp End of the Knife: Women as Mothers, Women as Writers." *Rendering Things Visible: Essays on South African Literary Culture.* Ed. Martin Trump. Athens: Ohio UP, 1990. 225-255.

Driver, Dorothy. "Women and Nature, Women as Objects of Exchange: Towards a Feminist Analysis of South African literature." *Perspectives on South African Literature.* Eds. Michael Chapman, Colin Gardner and Es'kia Mphahlele. Johannesburg: Ad. Donker, 1992. 454-474.

Eliot, George. *Felix Holt.* New York: J. W. Lovell, 1866.

Elphick, Richard. "Africans and the Christian Campaign in Southern Africa." *The Frontier in History: North America and Southern Africa Compared.* Ed. Howard Lamar and Leonard Thompson. New Haven and London: Yale UP, 1981. 270-307.

Elphick, Richard. *Khoikhoi and the Founding of White South Africa.* Johannesburg: Ravan, 1985.

Elphick, Richard and Hermann Gilliomee. *The Shaping of South African Society, 1652-1820.* Cape Town: Longman, 1979.

Ermarth, Elizabeth. "Fictional Consensus and Female Casualties." *The Representation of Women in Fiction.* Ed. Carolyn G. Heilbrun and Margaret R. Higonnet. Baltimore: Johns Hopkins UP, 1981. 1-18.

Escobar, A. "Discourse and Power in Development: Michel Foucault and the Relevance of his Work to the Third World." *Alternatives* 10, 3 (1984-5): 377-400.

Essop, Ahmed. *The Visitation.* Johannesburg: Ravan, 1980.

Essop, Ahmed. *The Emperor.* Johannesburg: Ravan 1984.

Ettin, Mark V. *Betrayals of the Body Politic: The Literary Commitments of Nadine Gordimer.* Charlottesville and London: UP of Virginia, 1992.

Farred, Grant. "'Not Like Women at All': Black Female Subjectivity in Lauretta Ngcobo's *And They Didn't Die.*" *Genders* 16 (1993): 94-112.

Fatton, Robert, Jr. *Black Consciousness in South Africa: The Dialectics of Ideological Resistance to White Supremacy.* Albany: SUNY Press, 1986.

Gardner, Susan. "A Feminist Critique of *The Grass is Singing* as a 'Moral Panic' Novel." *Social Dynamics* 10, 1 (1984): 52-56.

Gates, Henry Louis, Jr. *Black Literature and Literary Theory.* New York: Methuen, 1984.

Gates, Henry Louis Jr, ed. *'Race', Writing and Difference.* Chicago: U of Chicago P, 1986.

Gerard, Albert. *Contexts of African Literature.* Amsterdam, Atlanta, GA: Rodopi, 1990.

Gerhart, Gail. *Black Power in South Africa: The Evolution of an Ideology*. Berkeley: U of California P, 1978.

Gilbert, Sandra. "Costumes of the Mind: Transvestism as Metaphor in Modern Literature." *Critical Inquiry* 7 (1980): 391-418.

Giliomee, Hermann. "Processes in Development of the Southern African Frontier." *The Frontier in History: North America and Southern Africa Compared*. Ed. Howard Lamar and Leonard Thompson. New Haven: Yale UP, 1981.

Giliomee, H. and L. Schlemmer. *From Apartheid to Nation-Building*. Cape Town: OUP, 1989.

Ginwala, Frene. "Women and the Elephant: The Need to Redress Gender Oppression." *Putting Women on the Agenda*. Ed. Susan Bazilili. Johannesburg, Ravan, 1991.

Gittings, Chris. "Canada and Scotland: Conceptualizing Postcolonial Spaces." *Essays on Canadian Writing* 56 (1995): 135-161.

Goddard, Kevin and Charles Wessels. *Out of Exile: South African Writers Speak. Interviews with Albie Sachs, Lewis Nkosi, Mbuleleo Mzamane, Breyten Breytenbach, Dennis Brutus, Kereopetse Kgositsile*. Grahamstown: NELM, 1992.

Gool, Reshard. *Cape Town Coolie*. Toronto: Tsar, 1989.

Gorak, Irene E. "Olive Schreiner's Colonial Allegory: *The Story of an African Farm*." *Ariel* 23, 4 (1992): 53 -72.

Gordimer, Nadine. 1961. "The Novel and Nation in South Africa." *African Writers on African Writing*. Ed. G. D. Killam. London: Heinemann, 1973: 33-52.

Gordimer, Nadine. "Is There Nowhere Else Where We Can Meet." *The Soft Voice of the Serpent and Other Stories*. New York: Viking Press, 1962.

Gordimer, Nadine. *Occasion for Loving*. London: Jonathan Cape, 1963.

Gordimer, Nadine. *The Conservationist*. London: Jonathan Cape, 1974.

Gordimer, Nadine. *July's People*. New York: Penguin, 1981.

Gordimer, Nadine. *A Sport of Nature*. New York: Knopf, 1987.

Gordimer, Nadine. *My Son's Story*. London: Penguin, 1990.

Gordimer, Nadine. *None to Accompany Me*. Toronto: Penguin, 1994.

Gordimer, Nadine. *Writing and Being*. Cambridge, Mass.: Harvard UP, 1995.

Gordimer, Nadine. *The House Gun*. New York: Farrar, Straus and Giroux, 1988

Gray, Stephen. "Plaatje's Shakespeare." *English in Africa* (1977): 1-6.

Gray, Stephen. *Southern African Literature: An Introduction*. Cape Town: David Philip, 1979.

Gray, Stephen. "Third World Meets First World: The Theme of 'Jim Comes to Joburg' in South African English Fiction." *Kunapipi* 7, 1 (1985): 61-80.

Greenblatt, Stephen. "Culture." *Critical Terms for Literary Study*. 2nd ed. Frank Lentriccia and Thomas McClaughlin. Chicago: Chicago UP, 1995.

Griffiths, Gareth. "The Myth of Authenticity." *The Post-Colonial Studies Reader*. Ed. Bill Ashcroft, Gareth Griffiths and Helen Tiffin. London: Routledge, 1995.

Grosz, Elizabeth. "Irigaray's Notion of Sexual Morphology." *Reimagining Women: Representations of Women in Culture*. Ed. Shirley Neuman and Glennis Stephenson. Toronto: U T P, 1993: 182-195.

Gubar, Susan. "The Birth of the Artist as Heroine: (Re) Production, the Kunstlerroman Tradition, and the Fiction of Katherine Mansfield." *The Representation of Women in Fiction*. Ed. Carolyn G. Heilbrun and Margaret R. Higonnet. Baltimore: Johns Hopkins UP, 1981.

Gunner, Liz. "Songs of Innocence and Experience: Women as Composers and Performers of Izibongo, Zulu Praise Poetry." *Women and Writing in South Africa: a Critical Anthology*. Ed. Cherry Clayton. Johannesburg: Heinemann, 1989. 12–39.

Gunner, Liz. "Remaking the Warrior? The Role of Orality in the Liberation Struggle and Post-Apartheid South Africa." *Current Writing* 7, 2 (1995): 19-30.

Guy, Jeff. "Gender Oppression in Southern Africa's Precapitalist Societies." *Women and Gender in Southern Africa to 1945*. Ed. Cherryl

Walker. Cape Town: David Philip, 1990. 33-47.

Gwala, Mafika. "Review of Black Consciousness in South Africa: The Dialectics of Ideological Resistance to White Supremacy." *Research in African Literatures* 19, 1 (1988): 89-94.

Habib, Adam and Sanusha Naidu. "Was there a 'Coloured" and 'Indian' Vote?" Paper from the Bristol conference on Nationalism, Identity and Minority Rights, 16-19 September 1999. Politikon (November 1999). *Special Issue on Elections* (Journal of South African Political Studies Association.)

Hall, S., C. Critcher, T. Jefferson, J. Clarke, and B. Roberts. *Policing the Crisis, Mugging, the State, Law and Order*. London: Macmillan, 1978.

Hamilton, Caroline, ed. *The Mfecane Aftermath*. Johannesburg: Witwatersrand UP, 1995.

Hansson, Desiree. "Working Against Violence Against Women." *Putting Women on the Agenda*. Ed. Susan Bazilili. Johannesburg, Ravan, 1991. 180-193.

Harney, Stefano. *Nationalism and Identity: Culture and Imagination in a Caribbean Diaspora*. Kingston: UWI; London: Zed Books, 1996.

Hawley, John, ed. "Writing the Nation: Self and Country in the Post-Colonial Imagination." *Critical Studies* Vol 7. Amsterdam-Atlanta, GA: Rodopi, 1996.

Head, Bessie. *The Collector of Treasures*. London: Heinemann, 1977.

Head, Bessie. *Maru*. London: Heinemann Educational, 1972.

Head, Bessie. "Interview with Michelle Adler, Susan Gardner, Tobeka Mda and Patricia Sandler." *Between the Lines*. Ed. Craig Mackenzie and Cherry Clayton. Grahamstown: NELM, 1989.

Head, Dominic. *Nadine Gordimer*. Cambridge: CUP, 1994.

Head, Dominic. 1995. "Gordimer's *None to Accompany Me*." *Research in African Literatures* 26, 4 (1995): 46-57.

Heble, Ajay, Donna Palmateer Pennee and J. R. (Tim) Struthers, eds. *New Contexts of Canadian Criticism*. Peterborough: Broadview Press, 1997.

Heble, Ajay. "New Contexts of Canadian Criticism: Democracy, Counterpoint, Responsibility." *New Contexts of Canadian Criticism*. Eds. Ajay Heble, Donna Palmateer Pennee and J. R. (Tim) Struthers. Peterborough: Broadview Press, 1997. 78-97.

Heilbrun, Caroline G. and Margaret Higonnet, eds. *The Representation of Women in Fiction*. Baltimore: Johns Hopkins UP, 1983.

Heyns, Michiel. "Fathers and Sons: Structures of Erotic Patriarchy in Afrikaans Writing of the Emergency." *Ariel* 27, 1 (1996): 81-104.

Heywood, Christopher. *Aspects of South African Literature*. London: Heinemann, 1976.

Hofmeyr, Isobel. "We Spend our Years as a Tale that is Told." *Oral Historical Narrative in a South African Chiefdom*. London: Heinemann, 1994.

Homans, Margaret. *Bearing the Word: Language and Female Experience in Nineteenth-Century Women's Writing*. Chicago and London: U of Chicago P, 1986.

Hunter, Eva. "'We Have to Defend Ourselves': Women, Tradition and Change in Lauretta Ngcobo's *And They Didn't Die*." *Tulsa Studies in Women's Literature* 13, 1 (1994): 113-126.

Hutcheon, Linda. "The Canadian Postmodern: A Study of Contemporary English-Canadian Fiction." *Studies in Canadian Literature*. Toronto: OUP, 1988.

Hulme, Peter. "Including America." *Ariel* 26, 1 (1995): 117-123.

Irele, Abiola. *African Experience in Literature and Ideology*. London: Heinemann, 1981.

Irigaray, Luce. *This Sex Which Is Not One*. Transl. Catherine Porter with Carolyn Burke. Ithaca, NY: Cornell UP, 1985.

Jacobs, J. U. "The Blues: An Afro-American Matrix for Black South African Writing." *English in Africa* 16, 2 (1989): 3-18.

Jacobs, J. U. "Zakes Mda and the (South) African Renaissance: Reading *She Plays With Darkness*." Unpublished paper from EACLALS Conference in Tubingen, Germany, May 1999.

Jacobson, Dan. *A Dance in the Sun*. London: Weidenfeld and Nicolson,

1956.

Jacobson, Dan. *Introduction to The Story of an African Farm*. London: Penguin, 1971.

Jameson, Fredric. *The Political Unconscious: Narrative as a Socially Symbolic Act*. London: Methuen, 1981.

Janmohamed, Abdul. *Manichean Aesthetics: The Politics of Literature in Colonial Africa*. Amherst: U of Mass P, 1983.

Jochelsen, Karen. "Women, Migrancy and Morality: A Problem of Perspective." *Journal of Southern African Studies* 21, 2 (1995): 323-332.

Johnson, Barbara. "Metaphor, Metonymy and Voice in *Their Eyes Were Watching God*." *Black Literature and Literary Theory*. 205-219.

Jolly, Rosemary. *Colonization, Violence and Narration in White South African Writing: Andre Brink, Breyten Brevtenbach and J. M. Coetzee*. Athens: Ohio UP, 1996.

Jordan, A. C. *Towards an African Literature: The Emergence of Literary Form in Xhosa*. Berkeley: U of California P, 1973.

Joubert, Elsa. *The Long Journey of Poppie Nongena*. Johannesburg: Jonathan Ball, 1980.

Kandiyoti, Deniz. "Identity and Its Discontents: Women and the Nation." *Colonial Discourse and Postcolonial Theory*. Eds. Patrick Williams and Laura Chrisman. New York: Columbia UP, 1994. 376-391.

Kane-Berman, John. *Soweto: Black Revolt, White Reaction*. Johannesburg: Ravan, 1978.

Karodia, Farida. *A Shattering of Silence*. Oxford: Heinemann, 1993.

Keegan, Tim. *Rural Transformations in Industrializing South Africa: The Southern High Veld to 1914*. London: Macmillan, 1987.

Kemp, Amanda, Nozizwe Madlala, Asha Moodley and Elaine Salo. "The Dawn of a New Day: Redefining South African Feminism." *The Challenge of Local Feminisms: Women's Movements in Global Perspective*. Ed. Amrita Basu, with the assistance of Elizabeth McGrory. Boulder: Westview Press, 1995.

King, Bruce, ed. *The Later Fiction of Nadine Gordimer*. Basingstoke, Hampshire: Macmillan, 1993.

King, Bruce, ed. *New National and Post-colonial Literatures: An Introduction*. Oxford: Clarendon Press, 1996.

King, Thomas. "Godzilla Versus Postcolonial." *New Contexts of Canadian Criticism*. 241-248.

Kinsman, Diana. "'Hungry Wolves': The Impact of Violence on Rolong Life: 1823-1836." *The Mfecane Aftermath: Reconstructive Debates in Southern African History*. Ed. Carolyn Hamilton. Johannesburg: Witwatersrand UP, 1995.

Klugman, Barbara. "Women in Politics under Apartheid: A Challenge to the New South Africa." *Women and Politics Worldwide*. Ed. Barbara J. Nelson and N. Chowdhury. New Haven: Yale UP, 1994.

Knox, Alice. "Cross-Racial Couples in Nadine Gordimer's Later Novels." *Ariel* 27, 1 (1996): 63-80.

Kunene, Mazisi. "South African Oral Tradition." *Aspects of South African Literature*. Ed. C. Heywood. London: Heinemann, 1976. 24-53.

Kuzwayo, Ellen. *Call Me Woman*. Johannesburg: Ravan, 1985.

Kuzwayo, Ellen. Interview with Cherry Clayton. *Between the Lines: Interviews With Bessie Head, Sheila Roberts, Ellen Kuzwayo and Miriam Tlali*. Grahamstown: NEILM, 1989. 57-68.

La Guma, Alex. *A Walk in the Night and Other Stories*. 1962. London: Heinemann, 1968.

La Guma, Alex. *The Stone Country*. London Heinemann, 1967.

La Guma, Alex. *In the Fog of the Season's End*. London: Heinemann, 1972.

La Guma, Alex. *Time of the Butcherbird*. London: Heinemann, 1979.

Lamar, H. and L. Thompson, ed. *The Frontier in History: North America and South Africa Compared*. New Haven and London: Yale UP, 1981.

Landry, Donna and Gerald MacLean. *Materialist Feminisms*. Cambridge, Mass.: Blackwell, 1993.

Lazar, Karen. "'The Passing Away of the Old Regime': Change, 'Truth' and Sexuality in Gordimer's *None to Accompany Me*." *Current Writing* 7, 1 (1995): 105-116.

Legassick, Martin. "The Griqua, the Sotho-Tswana and the Missionaries, 1780-1840: The Politics of a Frontier Zone." Ph.D. diss. University of California, Los Angeles, 1970.

Legassick, Martin. "Legislation, Ideology and Economy in Post-1948 South Africa." *Journal of Southern African Studies* 1,1 (1974): 5-34.

Legassick, Martin. "The Northern Frontier to 1820: the Emergence of the Griqua People." *The Shaping of South African Society, 1652-1820*. Ed. Richard Elphick and Hermann Gilliomee. Cape Town: 1979.

Lentriccia, Frank and Thomas McLaughlin. *Critical Terms for Literary Study*. 2nd ed. Chicago: Chicago UP, 1995.

Lessing, Doris. *The Children Of Violence*. London: Panther, 1952.

Lessing, Doris. *The Four-Gated City*. New York: Knopf, 1969.

Lessing, Doris. *The Grass is Singing*. London: Granada, 1980.

Lessing, Doris. *Landlocked*. London: Panther, 1965.

Lessing, Doris. *Martha's Quest*. London: Panther, 1952.

Lessing, Doris. *A Proper Marriage*. London: Panther, 1954.

Lessing, Doris. *A Ripple From the Storm*. London: Panther, 1958.

Lockett, Cecily. "Miriam Tlali: The Fabric of Experience. A Critical Perspective on the Writing of Miriam Tlali." *Women and Writing in South Africa: A Critical Anthology*. Ed. Cherry Clayton. Johannesburg: Heinemann, 1989. 275–86.

Loomba, Ania. *Colonialism/Postcolonialism*. London: Routledge, 1998.

Mabandla, Brigitte. "Promoting Gender Equality in South Africa." *Putting Women on the Agenda*. Ed. Susan Bazilli. Johannesburg: Ravan, 1991. 75-81.

Mackenzie, Craig and Cherry Clayton. *Between the Lines: Interviews with Bessie Head, Sheila Roberts Ellen Kuzwayo and Miriam Tlali*. Grahamstown: NEILM, 1989.

Mamdani, Mahmood. *Citizen and Subject: Contemporary Africa and the Legacy of Late Colonialism.* Princeton, NJ: Princeton UP, 1996.

Manicom, Linzi. "Ruling Relations: Rethinking State and Gender in South African History." *Journal of African History* 33 (1992): 441-465.

Manicom, Linzi. "Claiming our Rights as Women: Issues of Gender and Democracy in the New South Africa." *Democracy, Globalization and Transformation in Southern Africa.* Ed. Linda Freeman. Montreal: CRCSA Occasional Papers Vol. 1 (1996): 43-54.

Mannoni, O. *Prospero and Caliban: The Psychology of Colonization.* Transl. by Pamela Powesland. Foreword Philip Mason.

Marcus, Jane. "Liberty, Sorority, Misogyny." *The Representation of Women in Fiction.* Eds. Caroline G. Heilbrun and Margaret Higonnet. Baltimore: Johns Hopkins Press, 1981.

Marks, Shula and Anthony Atmore. *Economy and Society in Preindustrial South Africa.* London: Longman, 1980.

Marks, Shula and Stanley Trapido. *The Politics of Race, Class and Nationalism in Twentieth Century South Africa.* Harlow. Essex: Longman, 1987.

Mashinini, Emma. *Strikes Have Followed Me All My Life: A South African Autobiography.* 1989. New York: Routledge, 1991.

Magona, Sindiwe. *Living, Loving, and Lying Awake at Night.* 1991. New York: Interlink Books, 1994.

Magona, Sindiwe. *To My Children's Children.* 1990. New York: Interlink Books, 1994.

Magona, Sindiwe. *Forced to Grow.* New York: Interlink Books, 1998.

Matsikidze, Isabella. "Beyond Revolution: Nationalism and the South African Woman Author." *Writing the Nation: Self and Country in the Post-Colonial Imagination. Critical Studies* Vol. 7. Amsterdam-Atlanta, GA: Rodopi, 1996.

May, Brian. "Back to the Future: History in/and the Postcolonial Novel." *Introduction to Studies in the Novel* 29, 3 (1997): 267273.

Mbembe, Achille. "Provisional Notes on the Postcolony." *Africa* 62, 1 (1992): 3-37.

McDonald, Larry. "I Looked for It and There It Was – Gone: History in Postmodern Criticism." *Essays on Canadian Writing* 56 (1995): 37-50.

McClintock, Anne. "The Angel of Progress: Pitfalls of the Term 'Post-colonialism.'" *Social Text* 31-32 (1992): 1-15.

McClintock, Anne. *Imperial Leather: Race, Gender and Sexuality in the Colonial Contest*. New York: Routledge, 1995.

Mda, Zakes. *She Plays With the Darkness*. Florida Hills, SA: Vivlia, 1995.

Mda, Zakes. *Ways of Dying*. Florida Hills, SA: Vivilia, 1995.

Meli, Francis. *A History of the ANC: South Africa Belongs To Us*. Harare: Zimbabwe Publishing House, 1988.

Memmi, Albert. *The Colonizer and the Colonized*. Trans. Howard Greenfeld. New York: Orion, 1965.

Mhlophe, Gcina. "Nokulunga's Wedding." *Raising the Blinds: A Century of Writing by Women*. Johannesburg: Ad. Donker, 1990. 123-129.

Millin, S. G. *God's Step-Children*. 1924. Johannesburg: Ad. Donker, 1986.

Mitchell, Juliet. *Psychoanalysis and Feminism*. New York: Vintage, 1975.

Moyana, T. T. "Problems of a Creative Writer in South Africa." *Aspects of South African Literature*. Ed. C. Heywood. London: Heinemann, 1976. 85–98.

Mphe, Phaswane. "'Naturally These Stories Lost Nothing by Repetition': Plaatje's Mediation of Oral History in *Mhudi*." *Current Writing* 8, 1 (1996): 75-89.

Mphahlele, Ezekiel. *The African Image*. London: Faber and Faber, 1962.

Mphahlele, Ezekiel. "Prometheus in Chains – The Fate of English in South Africa." *The English Academy Review* 2 (1984): 89-104.

Munger, Edwin S. *Afrikaner and African Nationalism: South African Parallels and Parameters.* London: OUP, 1967.

Munro, Alice. *Open Secrets.* Toronto: Penguin, 1995.

Mzamane, Mbulelo. T*he Children of Soweto: A Trilogy.* Johannesburg: Ravan, 1982 .

Mzamane, Mbulelo. "The Uses of Traditional Oral Forms in Black South African Literature." *Literature and Society in South Africa.* Eds. Landeg White and Tim Couzens, Cape Town: Maskew Miller, 1984.

Mzamane, Mbulelo. "Sharpeville and its Aftermath: The Novels of Richard Rive, Peter Abrahams, Alex la Guma and Lauretta Ngcobo." *Ariel* 16, 2 (1985): 31-44.

Murray, Martin. *The Revolution Deferred: The Painful Birth of Post-Apartheid South Africa.* London: Verso, 1994.

Mvula, Kefiloe Tryphina. "The Naked Night." *Women in South Africa: From the Heart–An Anthology.* Johannesburg: Seriti sa Sechaba, 1988. 45-51.

Ndebele, Njabulo. *Fools and Other Stories.* 1983. London: Longman, 1998.

Ndebele, Njabulo. "The Rediscovery Of the Ordinary." *Perspectives on South African Literature.* 434-453.

Ndebele, Njabulo. *South African Literature and Culture: Rediscovery of the Ordinary.* With intro. by Graham Pechey. Manchester: Manchester UP, 1994.

Newman, Judie. *Nadine Gordimer.* London and New York: Routledge, 1988.

Ngcobo, Lauretta. "The African Woman Writer" and "My Life and My Writing." *A Double Colonization: Colonial and Post-Colonial Women's Writing.* Eds. K. H. Petersen and A. Rutherford. Mundelstrup: Dangaroo Press, 1986. 81-86.

Ngcobo, Lauretta. "A Black South African Writing Long After Schreiner." *The Flawed Diamond: Essays On Olive Schreiner.* Mundelstrup: Dangaroo Press, 1989.

Ngcobo, Lauretta. Introduction to *Footprints in the Ouag: Stories and Dialogues from Soweto*. Cape Town: David Philip, 1989.

Ngcobo, Lauretta. *And They Didn't Die*. New York : George Baziller, 1990.

Ngugi wa Thiong'o. *Decolonizing the Mind: The Politics of Language in African Literature*. London: James Currey, 1986.

Ngugi wa Thiong'o. *Moving the Centre: The Struggle for Cultural Freedoms*. London: James Currey, 1993.

Nhlapo, Thandabantu. "Women's Rights and the Family in Traditional and Customary Law." *Putting Women on the Agenda*. Johannesburg: Ravan, 1991. 111-123.

Nixon, Rob. *Homelands, Harlem and Hollywood: South African Culture and the World Beyond*. New York: Routledge, 1994.

Nkosi, Lewis. *Home and Exile*. London: Longmans, 1965.

Nkosi, Lewis. *Mating Birds*. New York: St. Martin's Press, 1986.

Nuttall, Sarah and Carli Coetzee, eds. *Negotiating the Past: The Making of Memory in South Africa*. Oxford: OUP, 1998.

Ogungbesan, Kolawole. "A Long Way from Vrededorp: The Reception of Peter Abrahams's Ideas." *Perspectives on South African Literature*. Eds . Michael Chapman, Colin Gardner, Es'kila Mphahlele. Johannesburg: Ad. Donker, 1992.

Parker, Kenneth, ed. *The South African Novel in English: Essays in Criticism and Society*. New York: Africana Publishing, 1978.

Paton, Alan. *Cry, the Beloved Country*. London: Jonathan Cape, 1948.

Paton, Alan. *Too Late the Phalarope*. New York: Scribner's, 1953.

Paton, Alan. *Towards the Mountain: An Autobiography*. New York: C. Scribner, 1980.

Paton, Alan. *Journey Continued: An Autobiography*. Oxford: OUP, 1988.

Paul, James. "Interview with Paul Carter." *New Literatures Review* 34 (Winter 1997): 9-26.

Pennee, Donna Palmateer. "Apres Frye, rien"? Pas du tout. From Contexts to New Contexts." *New Contexts of Canadian Criticism*. 202-219.

Plaatje, Sol T. *Native Life in South Africa*. 1916. With Foreword by Bessie Head and Intro. by Brian Willan. Harlow, Essex: Longman, 1987.

Plaatje, Sol T. *Mhudi*. 1930. With intro. by Tim Couzens, Johannesburg: Quagga Press, 1975.

Plomer, William. *Turbott Wolfe*. 1925. Johannesburg: Ad. Donker, 1980.

Preston, P. W. *Development Theory: An Introduction*. Oxford: Blackwell, 1996.

Qakisa, Mpine. "Storm on the Minedumps." *Women in South Africa: From the Heart–An Anthology*. Johannesburg : Seriti sa Sechaba, 1988. 154-160.

Ramphele, Mamphela with Chris MacDowell. *Restoring the Land: Environment and Chance in Post-Apartheid South Africa*. London: Panos, 1991.

Ranger, Terence. "Postscript: Colonial and Postcolonial Identities." *Postcolonial Identities in Africa*. Ed. Richard Werbner and Terence Ranger. London and New Jersey: Zed Books, 1996.

Reddy, Thiven. "The Politics of Naming: The Constitution of Coloured Subjects in South Africa." Unpublished paper, Bristol UK, conference on Nationalism, Identity, Minority Rights, 16-19 September, 1999.

Rex, John. Ethnic Minorities in the Modern Nation-State. *Working Papers in the Theory of MultiCulturalism and Political Integration*. Houndmills, Basingstoke: Macmillan, 1996.

Rex, John. "Theory of Race Relations: A Weberian Approach." *Sociological Theories, Race and Colonialism*. Paris: Unesco, 1980. 116-142.

Rich, Paul. "Tradition and Revolt in South African Fiction: The Novels of Andre Brink, Nadine Gordimer and J. M. Coetzee." *Journal of Southern African Studies* 9, 1 (October 1982): 54-73.

Rive, Richard, ed. *Olive Schreiner Letters: 1871-99.* With historical research by Russell Martin. Cape Town: David Philip, 1987.

Roberts, Sheila. "At a Distance: Dan Jacobson's South African Fiction." *Perspectives on South African English Literature.* Eds. Michael Chapman, Colin Gardner and Es'kia Mphahlele. Johannesburg: Ad. Donker, 1992. 213-220.

Rutherford, Anna, Lars Jensen and Shirley Chew. eds. *Into the Nineties: Post-Colonial Women's Writing.* Mundelstrup: Dangaroo Press, 1994.

Sachs, Albie. "Preparing Ourselves for Freedom." *Spring Is Rebellious: Arguments about Cultural Freedom by Albie Sachs and Respondents.* Eds. Ingrid de Kok and Karen Press. Cape Town: Buchu Books, 1990.

Said, Edward. *Orientalism: Western Conceptions of the Orient.* 1978. Harmondsworth : Penguin, 1987.

Said, Edward. *Culture and Imperialism.* New York: Knopf, 1993.

Sarup, Madan. *An Introductory Guide to Post-Structuralism and Postmodernism.* 1983. Athens: U of Georgia P, 1993.

Sassoon, Anne S. *Women and the State in Africa.* Boulder: Lynne Rienner Publishers, 1989.

Scott, Joan. *Gender and the Politics of History.* New York: Columbia UP, 1988.

Schreiner, Olive. *The Story of an African Farm.* London: Chapman-Hall, 1883; London: Penguin, 1971; Johannesburg: Ad. Donker, 1986.

Schreiner, Olive. *Thoughts on South Africa.* 1923. Introduced and annotated by M. Lenta. Johannesburg: Ad. Donker, 1992.

Schreiner, Olive. *From Man to Man.* London: Virago, 1926.

Schulze-Engler, Frank. "Literature and Civil Society in South Africa." *Ariel* 27, 1 (1996): 21-40.

Schulze-Engler, Frank. "The Politics of Postcolonial Theory." *Postcolonial Theory and the Emergence of a Global Society. ACOLIT* Special Issue No. 3 (1998). Eds. G. Collier, D. Riemenschneider, and F. Schulze-Engler. 31–35.

Sepamla, Sipho. *A Ride on the Whirlwind.* London: Heinemann, 1981.

Sepamla, Sipho. *Third Generation.* Johannesburg: Skota Ville, 1986.

Sepamla, Sipho. *A Scattered Survival.* Braamfontein: Skotaville, 1989.

Serote, Mongane. *To Every Birth Its Blood.* London: Heinemann, 1981.

Sisk, T. D. *Democratization in South Africa: The Elusive Social Contract.* 1995.

Singh, Ansuyah R. *Behold the Earth Mourns.* Johannesburg: CNA, 1960.

Slemon, Stephen. "Unsettling the Empire: Resistance Theory for the Second World." *New Contexts of Canadian Criticism.* 228-240.

Smit, Johannes A., Johan Van Wyk and Jean-philippe Wade. *Rethinking South African Literary History.* Berea, Durban: Y Press, 1996.

Smith, Pauline. *The Beadle.* London: Jonathan Cape, 1926.

Smith, Pauline. *The Little Karoo.* London: Jonathan Cape, 1925.

Sole, Kelwyn. "The Days of Power: Depictions of Politics and Community in Four Recent South African Novels." *Research in African Literatures* 19, 1 (1988). 65-88.

Sole, Kelwyn. "Democratizing Culture and Literature in a 'New South Africa': Organization and Theory." *Current Writing* 6, 2 (1994): 1-37.

Sole, Kelwyn. "South Africa Passes the Posts." *Alternation* 4, 1 (1997): 116-151.

Soyinka, Wole. *Myth, Literature and the African World.* Cambridge: CUP, 1976.

Slovo, Joe. "South Africa – No Middle Road." *Southern Africa: The New Politics of Revolution.* Eds. Basil Davidson, Joe Slovo and Anthony R. Wilkinson. Harmondsworth: Penguin, 1976. 105-210.

Spivak, Gayatri. "Can the Subaltern Speak?" *The Post-Colonial Studies Reader.* Eds. Bill Ashcroft, Gareth Griffiths and Helen Tiffin. London: Routledge, 1995. 24-28.

Stratton, Florence. *African Literature and the Politics of Gender.* London: Routledge, 1994.

Taylor, Charles. "The Politics of Recognition." *New Contexts of Canadian Criticism.* 98-131.

Thompson, Leonard. *The Political Mythology of Apartheid.* New Haven, Yale UP, 1985.

Thompson, Leonard. *A History of South Africa.* Revised ed. New Haven : Yale UP, 1995.

Thornton, Robert. "The Potentials of Boundaries in South Africa: Steps Towards a Theory of the Social Edge." *Postcolonial Identities in Africa.* 136-162. .

Tlali, Miriam. *Amandla.* Johannesburg: Ravan 1981.

Tlali, Miriam. "Detour into Detention." *Mihloti.* Johannesburg: Skotaville, 1984.

Tlali, Miriam. *Footprints in the Ouag.* Cape Town: David Philip, 1989.

Tlali, Miriam. *Muriel at Metropolitan.* Harlow, Essex: Longman, 1979

Touraine, A. *The Return of the Actor.* Minneapolis: Minneapolis UP, 1988.

Trump, Martin, ed. *Rendering Things Visible.* Johannesburg: Ravan Press, 1990.

Van der Post, Laurens. *In a Province.* London: Hogarth, 1934.

Van Vuuren, Willem. "African Nationalism and Nation-Building in South Africa." Outline of draft paper for Bristol, UK, Conference on Nationalism, Identity, Minority Rights" 16-19 September 1999.

Van Zanten Gallagher, Susan. *A Story Of South Africa: J. M. Coetzee's Fiction in Context.* Cambridge, Mass.: Harvard UP, 1991.

Van Zanten Gallagher, Susan. "The Backward Glance: History and the Novel in Post-Apartheid South Africa." *Studies in the Novel* 29, 3 (1997): 377–95.

Visser, N. W. "South Africa: The Renaissance that Failed." *Research in African Literatures* 11 1 (1976): 42-57.

Visser, N. W. "Censorship and Literature." *Perspectives on South African English Literature.* Eds. Michael Chapman, Colin Gardner, Eskia Mphahlele. Johannesburg: Ad. Donker, 1992. 484-496.

Visser, N. W. "Fictional Projects and the Irruptions of History: Mongane Wally Serote's *To Every Birth its Blood*." *Perspectives On South African Literature*. Eds. Michael Chapman, Colin Gardner and Es'kia Mphahlele. Johannesburg: Ad. Donker, 1992. 422-433.

Vivan, Itala, ed. *The Flawed Diamond: Essays on Olive Schreiner*. Mundelstrup: Dangaroo Press, 1989.

Voss, A. E. "A Generic Approach to the South African Novel in English." *UCT Studies in English* 7 (1977): 110-11.

Voss, A. E. "Avatars of Waldo." *Alternation* 1, 2 (1994): 15-25.

Wade, Jean-Philippe. "Peter Abrahams's *The Path of Thunder*: The Crisis of the Liberal Subject." *English in Africa* 16, 2 (1989): 61-75.

Wade, Michael. *Peter Abrahams*. London: Evans Bros, 1972.

Wade, Michael. *White On Black in South Africa: A Study of English Language Inscriptions of Skin Colour*. New York: St Martin's Press, 1993.

Wagner, Kathrin. *Rereading Nadine Gordimer*. Bloomington and Indianapolis: Indiana UP, 1994.

Walder, Dennis. *Post-Colonial Literatures in English: History, Language, Theory*. Oxford: Blackwell, 1998.

Walker, Cherryl. *Women and Resistance in South Africa*. London: Onyx Press, 1982.

Walker, Cherryl, ed. *Women and Gender in Southern Africa to 1945*. Cape Town: David Philip, 1990.

Walker, Cherryl. "Conceptualizing Motherhood in Twentieth Century South Africa." *Journal of Southern African Studies* 21, 3 (1995): 417-437.

Walker, Cherryl. "Gender and the Development of the Migrant Labour System, c. 1850-1930." *Women and Gender in Southern Africa to 1945*. 68-196.

Werbner, Richard. "Introduction: Multiple Identities, Plural Arenas." *Postcolonial Identities in Africa*. 1-26.

Werbner, Richard and Terence Ranger, eds. *Postcolonial Identities in Africa*. London: Zed Books, 1996.

White, Hayden. *The Content of the Form: Narrative Discourse and Historical Representation*. Baltimore: Johns Hopkins Press, 1987.

White, Landeg and Tim Couzens, eds. *Literature and Society in South Africa*. Cape Town: Maskew Miller Longman, 1984.

Wicomb, Zoe. *You Can't Get Lost in Cape Town*. London: Virago, 1987.

Willan, Brian. *Sol T. Plaatie: South African Nationalist 1876-1932*. London: Heinemann, 1984.

Williams, Raymond. *The English Novel from Dickens to Lawrence*. New York: OUP, 1970.

Willis, Susan. "Eruptions of Funk: Historicizing Toni Morrison." *Black Literature and Literary Theory*. 263-283.

Worsfold, Brian. "Black South African Country Women in Lauretta Ngcobo's Long Prose Works." *Altered State? Writing and South Africa*. Eds. E. Boehmer, L. Chrisman and K. Parker. Mundelstrup: Dangaroo Press, 1994.

Young, Robert. *Colonial Desire: Hybridity in Theory, Culture and Race*. London: Routledge, 1995.

Yudelman, David. *The Emergence of Modern South Africa: State, Capital and the Incorporation of Organized Labour on the South African Goldfields, 1902-1939*. Westport, Conn.: Greenwood Press, 1983.

Zamora, Lois Parkinson. "Allegories of Power in the Fiction of J. M. Coetzee." *Journal of Literary Studies* 2, 1 (1986): 1-14.

Biographical Note

Ann Clayton was a Lecturer in Commonwealth Literature at the University of Guelph and a Visiting Professor at the University of Waterloo. She was previously an Associate Professor of Literature at Rand Afrikaans University and a Lecturer at the University of the Witwatersrand in Johannnesburg, South Africa. She has also worked as a writer, freelance journalist and book reviewer.

Her critical articles on literature, arts, culture, and politics have appeared in South African, Canadian and international newspapers and journals. She has published several book-length academic titles: *Olive Schreiner: A Casebook* (McGraw-Hill), *Women and Writing in South Africa: A Critical Anthology* (Heinemann), *Olive Schreiner* (Twayne), and *Speaking of Wtiting: Conversations with Canadian Novelists* (Vocamus Community Publications). She has also published three volumes of poetry: *Leaving Home* (Red Kite / Snailpress), *Eternal Day* (Drum Media) and *Migration* (Vocamus Community Publications).

Since leaving academia, she has worked as a communications consultant for the Federal Government of Canada, working on parliament and policy-making, economic and social justice, women's equality, and international development.

www.ingramcontent.com/pod-product-compliance
Lightning Source LLC
Chambersburg PA
CBHW032255150426
43195CB00008BA/462